RECLAIMING LIFE

A GUIDE FOR PARENTS OF CHRONICALLY ILL CHILDREN

MAUREEN MICHELE, MD

RECLAIMING LIFE: A GUIDE FOR PARENTS OF CHRONICALLY
ILL CHILDREN

© Copyright 2022 Maureen Michele, MD

For more information, email team@maureenmichelemd.com

ISBN (paperback): 979-8-88759-217-6

ISBN (eBook): 979-8-88759-218-3

DOWNLOAD A FREE WORKBOOK!

To say thanks for purchasing my book, I would like to give you a free workbook that will accompany the book.

The book is filled with stories and learning. This workbook will allow you to journal and start practicing the lessons taught in the book.

I'd love for you to enjoy this for free.

maureenmichelemd.com/reclaiminglife

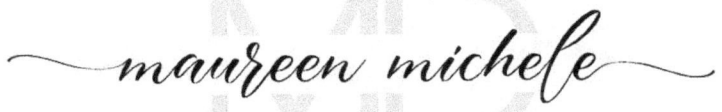

LEADER. PHYSICIAN. LIFE COACH

DEDICATION

To my children who taught me courage, compassion, and authenticity.
I am proud to be your mom.

To my patients who taught me the art of medicine.
I am honored to have been your doctor.

To my BFAL.
I am grateful you never stopped believing in me.

To my coach and friend.
I am grateful for your help in changing my life.

There once was a girl who wrote a book
To help parents who were overwhelmed and shook
But the message she wanted to say
Was don't let anything get in the way
Follow your dreams and let your joy be off the hook!

TABLE OF CONTENTS

FOREWARD

I had two dreams when I was young: 1) to be a mom and 2) to be a pediatrician. As a young child, I had several baby dolls that I loved as if they were real. I swaddled them in baby blankets, fed them with bottles, and changed their diapers. My bedtime routine was brushing my teeth, reading a book, and of course, rocking the dolls to sleep. My motherly instincts also made me worry about the health of my "babies." This concern for their well-being grew into pretending to be a doctor and using candy dots stuck on paper as "medicine" to dispense to my simulated childhood patients. My future aspirations were even obvious during childhood board games with neighborhood friends. I remember playing the game of LIFE™ and trying to rig the game to gather multiple little "peg" children to place in my game piece. When it was time to draw an occupation card, my heart raced as I crossed my fingers hoping I would draw the doctor card. This internal fire that was so present in my childhood continued motivating me to make my dreams a reality.

My dreams became reality when I walked across the stage on my father's fiftieth birthday and received my medical degree while pregnant with my first child. Over the next few years, I was blessed to become a mom on three separate occasions. Each child brought incredible joy and difficult challenges. However, navigating the health concerns of my children through the years brought the opposite: incredible challenges and difficult joy.

The word "parent" is derived from the Latin word *parentem* which means "to bring forth". This appropriately describes my role as a mother since I physically brought forth my children into this world. The word also represents the self-transformation stimulated by parenting. I was personally brought forth through my experience of parenting my children through their health journeys and became a loving, present mother and resilient, confident leader. From the beginning of my daughter's medical conditions, I learned lessons about managing my thoughts and mind. As time went on, my lessons included the importance of processing emotions, and lessons involving gratitude and celebration were learned and reinforced later in the journey. This book follows each stage in the journey—thoughts when I was consumed by negative thinking, emotions when I felt despair and fear, and actions and results when I learned to be grateful and celebrate the future. I will share experiences both as a mother and a physician to highlight individual lessons helping you bring forth your personal transformation.

I have two days that are etched in my brain. Those two days were "initiation days" into the club of parents with chronically ill children. I once read that when something traumatic happens, the moments of that day are etched in your brain, and they are difficult to erase from memory. Any time I speak about those days, I can see, hear, smell, and feel every single detail. At first, I thought it was a curse, but I now realize those are two days that helped me grow as a human. My memory of them is a blessing and serves as a reminder of how far I have come.

The club of parents with chronically ill children was not a club I asked to join. It was a club that was forced upon me. It is not a popular club, and it doesn't have a waitlist, but it does have an initiation fee which requires payment in the form of tears. I paid the fee and now I'm a lifelong member of the club. I have paid the annual dues of tears over and over again. Through the years, I learned that I can survive in this club while also being able to thrive. It no longer defines me, but instead it has made me into the strong, compassionate person I am today. I hope that you, too, can learn to thrive by incorporating the lessons of my journey.

If you are new to the club, welcome! If you are already a life-long member of the club, have no fear because you are not alone! I hope my experience can bring you hope that your life as a parent can be full and rewarding despite your child's health needs. Life is sometimes challenging, but it is through these moments that we become the best version of ourselves.

xo,

Maureen Michele, MD

Thoughts

Chapter 1

FOUNDATION OF RESILIENCE

> *"Your mind is the basis of everything that you experience and of every contribution you make to the lives of others. Given this fact, it makes sense to train it."*
> *– Sam Harris*

As human beings, we are fortunate to have an incredible tool that helps us find solutions, be creative, and contribute to humanity—our brain. Our brain offers us tens of thousands of thoughts every single day with some of these thoughts being intentional and necessary. Other thoughts, though, are fleeting and unintentional, appearing from our subconsciousness. The role of our primitive brain is to offer thoughts that keep us safe and accept the status quo. For example, when our brain offers the thought of, *This is hard*, it is trying to make sure there is inaction knowing risk is involved in taking new action.

The foundation of resilience is consciousness of our thoughts. As a pediatrician, I witnessed the impulsivity of small children. While a child tore up the exam table paper or pulled countless ear speculums out of the holder, the parents often were unaware of the child's crazy, destructive actions because their attention was elsewhere. To manage that child, the parent first needed to become aware of what the child was doing and then the parent could take the steps to guide the child. This is similar to our brain. Our brain requires the same parental supervision as a young child in the doctor's office.

Consciousness of our thoughts is not an easy skill because of how quickly our brain provides more thoughts. Our minds race with a plethora of thoughts, especially during times of perceived crisis. Sometimes unproductive thoughts loop in our mind and slowing the mind become necessary. Science has shown that focusing on breathing provides stillness of the mind. If you are focused on your breath, it is impossible to have chaotic thoughts because your brain cannot focus on different things simultaneously.

As we become aware of the thoughts in our mind, we can begin to provide supervision. A parent observing a small child in a doctor's office, first thinks about why the child is tearing the exam paper or why the child is removing the ear speculums. The parent's curiosity might bring understanding that the child is bored, or the child loves the sound of the crinkly paper. This understanding helps the parent provide alternative, less destructive activities. We can do the same for our thoughts. Questioning our thoughts with compassion and curiosity provides us with an understanding that helps us find thoughts to move us forward rather than continuing to believe the thoughts that keep us stuck.

Building resilience means we put order to the chaos of our mind. I was commissioned into the Army upon college graduation and the military helped me reach my dream of becoming a doctor. As a military physician and officer, I learned to understand the importance of order. Military formations provide the ability to achieve a mission in a unified way. Similarly, we need the child's cooperation in the doctor's office to avoid chaos and achieve the mission of behaving in the office. In the military, each member of the unit is focused on their role to overcome the enemy and this strategic organization helps decrease the risk of casualties that can occur when there is chaos. Consciousness and supervision of our thoughts allow us to declutter the chaos of our brain so we can maintain focus on accomplishing the mission.

Learning Thoughts Of Resilience Through Kyleigh

The birth of Kyleigh was surreal. My pregnancy with Kyleigh wasn't overly difficult and she was quick to make an appearance in the world following a relatively brief labor. She was my second child but seeing my baby girl for the first time took my breath away. I felt a sense of peace, along with excitement and intense love. With ten fingers, ten toes, a smidge of brown hair, and a beautiful set of blue eyes, my heart was grateful for this tiny creature. Jake was eighteen months old at the time and I could not wait for him to meet his sister.

Kyleigh's grandmother brought him to the hospital room and his dad held him over the warmer on which Kyleigh was resting. In his little voice, Jake hollered, "KY-EEE!". That little voice attempting to say her name brought me to tears. Jake came over to me as I was lying in the hospital bed and with him sitting next to me, I said, "It's Ky-Lee not Ky-Eee." There was joy in hearing Jake mispronounce Kyleigh's name that represented the pure innocence of his toddler years. Sadly, I knew that it wouldn't be long before his toddler's innocence would be gone, and he would be pronouncing her name correctly.

Unfortunately, the joy of Kyleigh's birth was short-lived. I knew something was wrong with Kyleigh when she was about three months old. She was having loose stools and we were changing diapers more frequently than I had with Jake. Even though I was only a third-year pediatric resident, my doctor brain kicked in and began creating a list of possible diagnoses—breast-feeding stools, viral gastroenteritis, parasitic infection, and milk-protein allergy. I was a doctor who would take care of sick children, but not *have* sick children. I believed my profession would protect me from being on the patient side of medicine. I knew it couldn't be anything too serious because I had the magic doctor card.

Kyleigh's pediatrician was my fellow resident and friend. I mentioned my concern in passing and he, too, was stumped. He agreed with my list of possible diagnoses and suggested that we get the opinion of our pediatric GI doctor. The GI physician evaluated Kyleigh by looking at her growth chart, doing an exam, and testing her stools. Because her test was positive for blood, I was relieved to find out that the diagnosis was just as I suspected—milk-protein allergy. I left the office with a plan to remove all dairy products from my diet and continue breastfeeding, using a special formula to supplement if needed. Infants usually outgrow this condition so I was hopeful that with time and avoidance of cow's milk, Kyleigh would be back to normal.

The diarrhea continued despite my efforts to maintain a strict dairy-free diet. I followed up with the GI physician and he wanted to perform an endoscopy procedure, hoping a biopsy of her gut tissue would lend clues to the problem. I was becoming more concerned since her symptoms hadn't resolved and wondered if we were really on the right track.

I agreed with the GI doctor's suggestion for an endoscopy and Kyleigh underwent the procedure, but unfortunately, the biopsies were all normal tissue. Some parents would be thrilled to hear the biopsies were normal, but I was left unsettled without evidence pointing to a diagnosis. The GI doctor explained that he still believed Kyleigh had milk-protein allergy and of course I agreed, because I am a doctor which protects me from having children with serious health problems. We decided to monitor her weight closely and reintroduce dairy products into my diet since it wasn't making a difference in her clinical symptoms. I knew he could not be wrong because of my magic doctor card.

January 19, 2001 was the day when I figured out that my magic doctor card had no real magic. Kyleigh was just a few weeks shy of her six-month birthday when I brought her into the clinic for a weight check. I placed her chubby body on the scale and realized her weight gain was good despite the ongoing GI issues. I was relieved to see her weight progressing as the nurse plotted the weight on the growth chart. I held Kyleigh and kept Jake in his stroller when the nurse took us back to my friend's office. My friend looked at the chart and reassured me that the numbers were increasing appropriately. He then said, "As long as you are here, let me do a quick exam. I want to take a quick listen to her heart and feel her belly."

Jake was too busy playing with a blown-up medical glove to care about the additional time in the pediatrician's office. "Sure!" I replied. My friend listened intently with Kyleigh on my lap and then he had me place her on the exam table. He felt her abdomen, paused, and then felt it again. He again paused and felt the left side of her belly another time. I noticed the repetition which I thought was odd, but I remained unconcerned since his face displayed a look of curiosity more than concern. He finished and told me that he was feeling something—he wasn't sure exactly what it was and wanted the opinion of one of the staff providers. The pediatrician left and brought the staff attending physician in, who proceeded to feel Kyleigh's belly. In the usual fashion of a physician, he rattled off a list of possible diagnoses like I had done in my own mind—hydronephrosis, Wilm's tumor, multicystic kidney, and others, but all I heard was "normal kidney," so I wasn't worried.

Jake was now entertaining himself by trying on hospital gloves and tossing around his hospital glove balloon like a hot potato while he sat in his stroller. We left the office with the staff attending physician arranging for us to be at radiology a few hours later so they could perform an ultrasound to get further evidence on what this physical exam finding could be. This seemed like a silly plan to waste time and resources imaging a normal kidney, but I didn't object and arrived at radiology at the appointed time.

Kyleigh and I waited to be called from the radiology waiting area while entertaining Jake who continued to sit his stroller next to us. A young technician came out to the waiting room and boldly announced, "Kyleigh Petersen." It was our turn, so I gathered our things, stood up with Kyleigh and pushed the stroller toward the woman. She smiled and calmly told us to follow her. We went into a dark room that contained a large ultrasound machine and an exam table. Immediately, the reality of the situation rushed over me, and I began getting nervous. I knew doctors didn't do ultrasounds on normal kidneys. Nervously, I parked the stroller in the corner of the room, not realizing Jake was within reach of a hospital glove box hanging from the wall. The young technician asked me to undress Kyleigh and place her on the table.

I stood back as the ultrasound technician did her work. She squeezed warm jelly over Kyleigh's belly and ran a probe through the jelly. I remember thinking how ridiculous Kyleigh looked on the table. Her tiny body clothed in only a diaper was barely taking up any space on that cold and sterile table with white paper pulled over the top. This was such a contrast to Kyleigh's warm and lively little body. My thoughts quickly shifted when the room suddenly filled with people—two pediatric radiologists, the staff attending pediatrician, my resident friend, and a few others I didn't recognize. They crowded around the ultrasound machine after quickly acknowledging me, since I was busy trying to prevent Jake from removing every single glove from the box on the wall.

The ultrasound tech stared at the screen on the machine as she tweaked the probe on Kyleigh's belly. "This is what I'm seeing," she gently said as she pointed at the screen. The crowd of physicians was absolutely silent, focused on the screen. Was it silence because they weren't certain what they were seeing? No, it was silence because they knew exactly what they were seeing. I was a pediatric resident, not a radiologist, so I wasn't an expert on reading ultrasounds, but as I shifted my attention from Jake to the screen, I easily saw a dark blob that I knew shouldn't be on that black and white screen. My stomach dropped and tears started to flow. I didn't know exactly what everyone was seeing, but I knew it was bad. In that moment, I also knew that physicians held no magic cards that prevented them from joining the club of parents with chronically ill children.

Thoughts immediately rushed through my mind:

I don't want my daughter to die.

I don't know how I am going to manage being a doctor and mother.

I don't want my child to experience pain and suffering.

I don't want my child to be a patient.

I need to tell her dad.

I need to tell my family.

My family is so far away.

I can't do this without help from my family.

This can't be happening.

Why is this happening to me?

The "blob" on the screen was a 3–4 cm solid tumor on top of her kidney at the site of her adrenal gland. It was the size of a golf ball. I knew that a golf-ball tumor in a tiny infant body was bad. The location really meant only one thing—neuroblastoma. Kyleigh needed more tests to determine the extent of the tumor and if it had spread. I needed to wake up from this nightmare. I needed to don a resilient suit of armor, but this had to start with controlling my mind. I needed to figure out how to cope with all this news because my infant daughter depended on my resilience. This would start with consciousness of my thoughts.

Years later, I learned it is important to never let your resilient suit of armor rust. Kyleigh grew from a sickly infant to a focused, driven, happy twelve-year-old child. I loved spending time with all my children, but as a woman, I felt like I had a job to do when I spent time with my only daughter, Kyleigh. I needed to teach her strength. I needed to model confidence. I needed to demonstrate the importance of compassion. She was a straight A student and beautiful ballet dancer. We had periodic mother/daughter dates like shopping trips, home facials, and trips to the theater. One day I decided that adding a hiking trip along the Potomac River to the list of our special date activities would be perfect. I had hiked the Billy Goat Trail several times in the past and I was excited to share the scenery with Kyleigh. The hike is a moderate trail that involves climbing on rocks to reach amazing views of the flowing Potomac River as it charges below. It was beautiful sunny day, but not overly humid when we decided to hike the two-mile trail. I was prepared with a bottle of water, but I wasn't prepared for Kyleigh's lack of energy. Kyleigh was an athletic kid, so she always able kept up with me, but not on this day.

As we hiked, Kyleigh begged me to stop and continuously asked me for water. She finished the bottle during the first half of the hike so the stopping, the requests for water, and the complaints that she was thirsty had increased during the second half of the hike. I thought it was unusual but didn't make too much out of it. I guessed Kyleigh just had a bad night's sleep. "Come on! You're my tough girl!" I reminded her. We took photos of the beautiful scenery, enjoyed laughing together, and completed the hike without making too much out of her uncharacteristic requests for water.

The following weekend, Kyleigh and Jake participated in a retreat to prepare for confirmation, a Catholic sacrament they would receive a few months later. While the kids were away, I participated in a multi-day team race, and I oversaw supplying the sports drinks. After the race, I had lots of sports drinks remaining that I brought home and stuck in the fridge. When Jake and Kyleigh returned, they were surprised to see the sports drinks and were excited to have this unusual treat since I rarely bought them. Immediately, they each grabbed one out of the refrigerator and guzzled the drinks without even allowing time for me to stop the indulgence.

Later, I asked Kyleigh if she wanted to come with me down the street to the nail shop so we could get pedicures. Caring for her feet was important for her ballet so this trip down the street was not unusual. She needed to use the bathroom before we headed out of the house. After she was done, we drove down the street to the shop and arrived a minute or two later ready to pick out our polish color. As we stood at the counter, I noticed Kyleigh was wiggling as she debated between the available polish colors. She selected her polish and said, "Mom, I better go to the bathroom before they start." I told her to hurry, and I took my place in my assigned pedicure chair. She returned, sat in her chair, and watched intently as the nail technician worked on her feet.

After our polish was dry, I stood at the counter to pay for the services with Kyleigh standing next to me. She was wiggling again. She turned to me and said, "I need to pee again before we leave." With a bit of annoyance, I told her to hurry up and I would meet her at the car, but I couldn't help but wonder how many sports drinks she had to drink because of this frequent urination. When she returned to the car, she was adamant that she only had two. I paused and replayed the previous guzzling session in my mind like a movie. I knew Kyleigh was telling the truth, but how could that be? I backed the car out of the parking lot and headed home knowing she must have gotten excited and drank more than she realized.

Dinner wasn't anything special, but Kyleigh could not sit still. She visited the bathroom twice during dinner and wiggled in her seat throughout the meal.

When she returned, I put on my doctor's hat and began asking more questions. Her answers were unremarkable.

"Does it hurt when you pee?"

"No."

"Are you peeing just a little amount?"

"No, the normal amount."

"Any pain anywhere else?"

"No, I feel fine."

Puzzled I mumbled to myself, "I wonder if she has diabetes."

"Mom, what's diabetes?" Kyleigh asked.

We went through serious health issues already with Kyleigh so I was confident we couldn't be unlucky enough to have another problem. This confidence led me to believe that the diagnosis of diabetes couldn't be the real problem. I reassured Kyleigh as she went back to her meal. Years prior, I was certain my medical degree prevented me from having kids with a serious illness, but then Kyleigh had neuroblastoma. This could not be diabetes because I checked that box with Kyleigh's cancer diagnosis. I suspected Kyleigh had a urinary tract infection because that would be a common, easily treatable diagnosis that could explain some of her symptoms.

The following day, Kyleigh sent me a text message during her lunch period. The message simply read, "Mom, bring home whatever you need to bring to fix me. I peed twelve times today."

My suspicion was now confirmed. She clearly had a urinary tract infection, and I was glad that she was feeling fine otherwise, but I knew I needed to figure out how to treat this. The first step was confirming the diagnosis, so I decided to grab a urine cup and a urine dipstick from the pediatrics clinic to have Kyleigh give me a sample when I picked her up from school. This would allow me to bring her back to the hospital's pharmacy to get antibiotics before heading home. I walked to the pediatric clinic and a nurse colleague helped me grab the contraband supplies that I needed to be the pediatrician for my child.

When I arrived at Kyleigh's school, Kyleigh eagerly greeted me at the front desk asking if I brought what she needed. I had all the supplies and showed her the urine cup. I explained that she needed to go to the school bathroom and provide me with a urine sample. Kyleigh grabbed the cup and closed the bathroom door. A minute or two later, Kyleigh cracked the door open and told me to come in. I entered the small bathroom that had one toilet and a sink. Kyleigh handed me the cup that was filled with light colored urine, and I slowly dipped one of the urine test strips into the liquid. I pulled out the test strip with Kyleigh intently watching my every movement. I watched in horror as the glucose measurement on the dipstick quickly turned from a pale yellow to a very dark black color.

I felt like I was transported back to the ultrasound room when I had my first glimpse of the dark blob of neuroblastoma on the screen. Once again, my stomach dropped, and the tears started to flow. I took a breath since I knew I needed to form words to tell Kyleigh the news. "You have diabetes," I said shakily through my tears.

"Am I going to die?" Kyleigh asked.

"No, baby, you are not going to die," I replied.

Now Kyleigh was crying and through her tears she asked, "Then why are you crying?"

"Because I don't want you to have diabetes." I pulled her tight into a strong hug and we froze as our tears continued to flow.

In that tiny school bathroom, I joined the club again— even as a doctor and even as a parent with a child who had seemingly overcome cancer. I already knew I hated this club, but without being able to control my tears, I paid my dues for re-entry.

Thoughts once again came rushing through my brain.

This will change everything.

My child has already suffered.

I don't want my daughter to be poked.

I don't want Kyleigh to die.

This will be a huge challenge.

I cannot believe this is happening.

Why is this happening to me again?

We grabbed her things and rushed off to the car. As a pediatrician, I knew a patient with new onset diabetes needed to be admitted to the hospital and often the ICU. I nervously drove off to the hospital but tried to maintain my composure so Kyleigh wouldn't become nervous. At the emergency room, we waited patiently for the nurse to call us back for the evaluation.

When facing your child's new diagnosis, your brain might offer many thoughts just as mine did. I knew, once again, I needed to be resilient. As I rebuilt the foundation for resilience, I needed to be conscious and curious about my thinking.

When receiving bad news about our child, we can experience tremendous grief. In 1969, Dr. Elizabeth Kubler-Ross reported the five stages of grief: denial, anger, bargaining, depression, and acceptance. Parents who receive news of their child's chronic illness naturally enter each of these stages of grief. We grieve the loss of our old life and the life we envisioned. It becomes necessary to process the emotions associated with these stages of grief.

Being a doctor is an honor. I have watched children grow, heard stories of healing, and shed tears of sadness when death occurs. It is humbling to realize that my skills have changed the trajectory of many people's lives, but I often don't think about that. I do, however, spend time thinking about the families that joined the club, and I was the one who handed them their unrequested invitation.

I hate giving bad news. Not only do I hate it because bad news makes me sad, but I hate it because delivering bad news can bring conflict. More than my hatred of bad news, I hate conflict. But I found myself in a role that required me to deliver bad news as a physician. After spending a career in medicine, you would think I wouldn't mind it, but I still hate it. There is nothing good about delivering bad news.

I was a pediatric resident, called to be present at a newborn delivery because the obstetrician had a concern. A pregnant young woman was in the hospital bed with a man at the side of the bed holding her hand when I entered the room. She was in labor and ready to begin pushing. It wouldn't be long before she would become a mother. I don't remember the concern that made the obstetrician ask for help, but it was common because the birth of a child is a high-risk medical procedure. I could hear the woman pushing, along with words of encouragement from the man as I got the infant's warmer ready. I turned up the temperature of the warmer, checked the light on the laryngoscope, checked the size of the endotracheal tube, turned up the oxygen, made sure the bag to deliver breaths was working, and the suction was on. I had towels, blankets, and an infant hat. I was ready for my patient.

The obstetrician hollered, "It's a boy!" She handed the man surgical scissors to cut the umbilical cord and then quickly passed the infant off to me. I placed the baby boy on his back on the warmer I had prepared. I immediately initiated my newborn emergency medical care steps—dry, warm, position, suction, stimulate. These were the initial steps I took each time I attended a delivery, but this time was different.

As I was warm drying the infant, I immediately noticed his lower jaw was different. It was much smaller than normal and appeared recessed. His skin was pink, and he was crying which gave me comfort that his physical abnormality wasn't causing immediate concerns. He didn't need any immediate pediatric intervention, but as I continued to get him ready to meet his parents, I did a quick exam. My initial assessment about his jaw was accurate. His lower jaw was very small and recessed and I immediately knew the diagnosis—Pierre Robin syndrome. This is a syndrome where the infant's jaw is too small to support the infant's tongue. This syndrome often leads to obstructed breathing, feeding issues, and speech delays.

My stomach dropped. I would have to deliver a club invitation during a moment that was supposed to be the most joyous day for this family. I would have to welcome this family to the club of parents with chronically ill children during their precious moment.

I wrapped the baby and placed a hat on his head. He had stopped crying, but I was concerned he would stop breathing if I allowed him to stay on his back due the obstruction his tongue could cause. I brought the baby boy to his parents and placed him in the man's arms. I gently explained that the baby was doing great, but there was a problem with his jaw. I then gave the diagnosis and began explaining what it meant, including the need to closely monitor the infant in the Neonatal Intensive Care Unit until we knew he could comfortably breathe. The tears that were the initiation fee to join the club began flowing down the man and woman's cheeks. The man gave a simple reply, "His name is Harry."

Thoughts began filling my mind during this uncomfortable, stressful moment.

I hope they are able to adjust.

I just crushed their dream of this moment.

I don't think they understand the struggles ahead.

I need to keep this baby safe.

I want this child to get discharged quickly.

This child is facing an uphill journey.

This isn't fair.

Once again, the suit of armor of resiliency was needed, but this time I knew it would also be needed for the new parents who were initiated into the club. Harry had a challenging hospital course because he had tremendous difficulty eating due to the malformation of his jaw. We were all thrilled when he was successfully discharged home and I continued to care for him in our pediatric clinic. Harry's parents slowly built their armor, and humbly, I was there to support them knowing exactly how their parent brain was thinking.

Lessons On Resilience

Our brain's job is to think, and it accomplishes this duty by delivering many, many thoughts every day. Our thoughts make us feel, which drives our actions. It is understandable that our thoughts are very important when we are working toward a specific outcome in our life. Thoughts are the beginning of a powerful cascade. Thinking, though, is very different than awareness of thought. Changing the outcome of the cascade occurs when we change what initiated it, but we can only work to change what our mind is thinking when we are aware of our thoughts.

Imagine you were standing on a hill overlooking a very busy highway. The speed limit is seventy miles per hour, and you are watching as the cars whiz by. The stream of cars looks like a blur because they are going so fast, and you don't have time to focus on the details of the passing vehicles. This is thinking. Now imagine that you are standing on the hill, waving a flag to make the cars slow down. The cars slow to a crawl, and you notice some cars are blue and others are red with stripes. This is consciousness or awareness. This is a critical first step in building the foundation for resiliency.

Chaos. That is the word that best described my former life as a parent with a medically challenged child. The chaos came from the extra responsibilities needed to keep my kid healthy such as medical appointments, ordering supplies, and refilling medications on top of the typical life responsibilities of work and maintaining a household. Every day I was playing a game of whack-a-mole and never knew how my day would end, but I was certain I would never have time for myself, and I never did.

I woke up each morning trying to muster the strength to meet the challenges that I knew would face me that day. My first thought was always, *I wonder what fires I am going to put out today.* Each day ended with reflecting on the headaches I endured that day. I thought:

This was another bad day.

My days are crazy.

I can't get everything done.

There is too much on my plate.

I am stuck in this life.

My brain spent the night reflecting on these thoughts. Sleep was restless and I woke up stressed and unmotivated to get out of bed. I had no personal goals and I felt defeated before the day even started.

The thoughts made me feel terrible which caused me to sabotage life. I needed to become aware of my thoughts. I needed to wave the flag on the hill and pause to pay attention to the ideas my mind was creating. Negative thoughts destroying our resilience can be halted and changed, but only if consciousness occurs.

Our brain works to find evidence supporting the thoughts it is producing. If we think, *This was another bad day,* then our brain focuses on every bad thing that happened during the day. Our brain becomes blinded to the good things because that would not support the thought. This knowledge is exciting and provides parents with the possibility to improve their lives. If our brain's thought is, *This was a great day,* then our brain focuses on every good thing and it changes how we feel. The way we act during the day is the result of how we think and feel. Consciousness of our mind is a skill that needs to be practiced.

Steps to achieve consciousness of thoughts:

1. **WRITE DOWN YOUR THOUGHTS.** It is helpful to visualize your thoughts without judgment. Each time I faced a new diagnosis with Kyleigh, whether it be neuroblastoma or diabetes, I immediately thought, *I can't do this.* Writing it down took it out of my brain and made it exist as just words on a paper. Keeping it stuck in my head led to harsh criticism of myself with thoughts such as, *I am a terrible parent.*

2. **BE CURIOUS.** Adding curiosity gives us the ability to have a holistic view of our thinking. Is the thought even true? Objectively, we can consider both the evidence that proves the negative thought and the evidence that goes against the negative thinking. Seeing the words, "I can't do this," on the paper led me to be curious. I did lots of hard things in my life— was this thought even true? Probably not because I could only find evidence to demonstrate that I was very capable of overcoming challenges.

3. **DECIDE IF A THOUGHT NEEDS TO BE CHANGED.** "I can't do this," made me give up before even trying. I am a stubborn person who never gives up. This thought needed to be changed. "I can try to do hard things," was the new thought I chose to believe.

Going through this process and learning to change my thoughts significantly changed my life. My first thought when I wake up in the morning is, *Today is going to be a great day.* I spend quiet time in the morning meditating, journaling, and reading. I start my day feeling energized and calm. Each day now ends with thoughts such as:

This was a good day.

I can successfully manage my days.

Everything that needs to get done will be done.

My plate is full of the things I enjoy.

I love my life.

Fulfilling. That word best describes my current life, still as the mother of a child with chronic medical problems. I have goals I achieved and continue to work to achieve, including professional and personal goals. I have meaningful relationships with my children, significant other, friends, and colleagues. I am grateful for the life I was given. The things I have achieved have been the direct result of redirecting my brain and working to collect evidence to support my new and improved thoughts.

Changing our thinking is challenging and takes practice. When performing a push-up for the first time, the push-up will be slow and unsteady, and your arms will be sore. Our brain is similar when we begin practicing something new. At first, changing thoughts will be slow and difficult, but with practice, the skill becomes easier and requires less effort.

Building resiliency requires the four Cs: consciousness (awareness), curiosity, commitment, and courage. This practice takes time, but it is ultimately time well invested into being the best version of ourselves.

Chapter 2

COURAGE

> *"I learned that courage was not the absence of fear,*
> *but the triumph over it. The brave man is not he who*
> *does not feel afraid, but he who conquers that fear."*
> — *Nelson Mandela*

C ourage is the ability to find strength to drive actions during times of extreme adversity. It is the attribute needed to overcome fear to do something dangerous or challenging. Advocacy requires courage to disagree and negotiate when needed. Being a parent of a chronically ill child involves advocacy for our child and we must act despite initial feelings of doubt, fear, or discomfort.

The courage to advocate is intentionally deciding not to be held back. Often fear and doubt are what holds us back from being the best advocate. Fear and doubt are created by ideas our mind offers, just like any other emotion. The first step in controlling these emotions is being aware of the thoughts driving fear or doubt. Objectively evaluating a situation and identifying the reason behind the emotion being felt will allow us to control negative emotions and generate courage.

Standing in the ultrasound room with Jake in the stroller and Kyleigh naked on the exam table, both unaware of what was occurring, the diagnosis of neuroblastoma hit me like a strong punch to my gut. The days after the initial ultrasound were filled with a flurry of medical appointments. Kyleigh had to undergo a sedated MRI and a bone scan. She underwent a bone marrow biopsy and evaluation by a pediatric surgeon. We had a pre-op appointment to discuss the plan for anesthesia that would be best for the day of surgery. I was like a breathless zombie taking her from appointment to appointment.

All the work-up was looking positive. No metastasis in the bone or liver, which are the common sites where neuroblastoma spreads. The tumor was involving the left adrenal gland on top of the left kidney which was a tough location due to the proximity to large vessels, but the pediatric surgeon reassured us that the surgery would not take longer than two hours. Even though the official staging of the cancer could not be done prior to surgery, everyone was optimistic that it was stage 1 and surgery would be the only necessary treatment.

Kyleigh developed a cold the day prior and was up through the night with a cough and stuffy nose. As a physician, I knew this was not a good way to go into surgery. When a patient's lungs are already irritated by a virus, using anesthesia and undergoing an intubation would be risky. The lungs don't want more irritation. I tried everything to improve her symptoms overnight, including warm steam in the bathroom and vaporizing menthol patches for her chest. Nothing worked. What I really needed was a miracle.

The day of surgery was emotionally challenging. I dressed Kyleigh in her tiny hospital gown, picked her up, and held her tightly as I stood rocking her. I was afraid for the challenging road ahead, but even more anxious because I had no control over her survival. It was like I was standing in the door of a plane with a parachute on my back. I could see the ground below, but it was terrifying realizing it was so far away and all I could do was pray that my parachute would open to help me make it down safely.

The anesthesiologist entered to discuss the final plan for the operating room. I knew from being involved in the care of pediatric oncology patients that kids receive chemotherapy through a central line, a special catheter placed in a large vein. This was an important tool in pediatric oncology because it could be used to draw blood and administer medication like chemotherapy. It could prevent many blood-draw sticks and IV pokes, but it needed to be placed surgically in the operating room. No one had mentioned a central line, because no one was thinking chemotherapy would be necessary. I knew this was the moment I needed to advocate for my child. As I searched for words, I felt my worry bubbling. Was I going to be heard? What if the anesthesiologist disagreed? I knew I needed to gather my courage and speak up because the only thing that really mattered was Kyleigh's health. I looked at the anesthesiologist and told her if it looked worse than predicted and chemotherapy was going to be in the treatment plan, I was giving my permission to make sure they put in a central line, so Kyleigh didn't need to go back to the operating room. The anesthesiologist understood and agreed. Tremendous relief rushed over me, dispelling any concern I had about speaking up.

Handing my child over the anesthesiologist was one of the hardest things I had ever done. As a mother, I was supposed to be the one protecting my child. As a doctor, I was supposed to be the one fixing her pain. In that moment, I knew I could not fulfill either of those duties. I would be trusting another individual to watch over Kyleigh. The anesthesiologist turned to me as she was walking away with Kyleigh in her arms and said, "I will treat her like my own!" Those words brought me comfort, but it still felt like a piece of my heart was ripped out as I watched Kyleigh disappear down the sterile hallway.

The surgery took ten hours, not the anticipated two hours. I sat in the Pediatric Intensive Care waiting room with a bag full of pistachios and for ten hours, I cracked pistachios while saying prayers. I watched the PICU nurses flutter around caring for the other patients in the unit. At one point during the day, a woman in scrubs, surgical hat, and surgical shoe covers came into the PICU. She asked one of the PICU nurses if there was any pediatric transfusion tubing and filters in the PICU storage area. Together the PICU nurse and surgical woman found the tubing and the surgical woman raced away.

My stomach sank. Kyleigh was the only major pediatric surgery scheduled that day and the only other place that could need pediatric transfusion supplies was the pediatric ward. I knew all the nurses on the ward, but I did not know the woman in surgical attire. I knew this tubing was intended for Kyleigh. I was certain after a few moments of thought that the woman was an operating room nurse, and Kyleigh was getting a transfusion. Sure, they had spoken to me about this as a risk, but this was not supposed to happen. My thoughts began racing, guessing what was really happening in the operating room.

I told myself to be brave and kept waiting. My brain was on overdrive, providing me with thought after thought about every catastrophic thing that could be happening in the operating room. I once again needed my resilient suit of armor. Attempting to quiet my mind, I ate pistachios. Staying focused on cracking pistachios kept my hands busy and slowed the thoughts swirling in my mind.

Many hours later, Kyleigh finally arrived in the PICU late in the afternoon and she was struggling. I was filled with mixed emotions—exhaustion from hours of worry, relief that she was done with surgery, and helplessness from seeing her uncomfortable and struggling. Her small body was hooked to tubes and monitors, and she had an epidural in place to help with the pain. Her breathing tube was removed in the operating room, and she was now working very hard to breathe. The cold symptoms from the previous night along with the lengthy surgery resulted in a tremendous amount of airway irritation that forced Kyleigh to work for each breath.

The tumor was in a trickier position than originally anticipated, and lymph nodes along her aorta that were thought to be involved had to be left in place. She had received a transfusion due to the blood loss, but the surgery was a success. Kyleigh had no central line in place.

That night was challenging due to Kyleigh's discomfort, but the following day proved to be more of a challenge. Kyleigh's team of doctors came in the following morning and further discussed the surgery. The presumably involved lymph nodes changed the stage of her diagnosis. She was now stage IIIC. This meant the tumor was more serious and had grown and spread. This meant chemotherapy and back to the operating room for a central line. My efforts for advocacy failed. I was left feeling angry and unheard. I felt guilty because I knew my attempts to get a central line placed at the time of surgery wasn't for my convenience, it was for my daughter's health. Failing when someone is depending on you is a terrible feeling. I had failed my daughter.

Kyleigh's cancer care as an infant wasn't the only time I needed courage. After I diagnosed Kyleigh with diabetes in the school bathroom, Kyleigh and I wiped the tears from our face in the school bathroom, grabbed her school bags, and dashed to the car. The car ride to the hospital started as eerily quiet. Both of us were lost in our thoughts.

After softly sniffling, Kyleigh was the one who broke the silence and said, "Mom, I have two things that I want to make sure happen at the hospital."

"Ok, what's that sweetheart?" I replied.

"First, if they have anything to tell us, I want them to tell you first and you can tell me."

I quickly replied, "Kyleigh, they are not going to tell you anything we don't already know. The only surprise they could say is that you do not have diabetes, which would mean your mom is a moron. I am pretty sure I am not a moron, so nothing is going to be a surprise. What's the second thing?"

Kyleigh said, "I don't want anyone rushing."

I was puzzled. "What do you mean 'rushing?' I don't understand why you don't want anyone rushing."

"Mom," as the sniffling got louder, "every time that I've seen doctors on TV rush to take care of a patient, the patient dies. I don't want to die. Please no rushing."

Kyleigh had grown up around medicine. She came to clinic with me on countless occasions. She accompanied me on patient rounds on the inpatient ward. She walked around the hospital with me and probably even knew her way without assistance from me. As familiar as she was with medical stuff, this was not her profession. The words she said in that moment made me realize how terrified she was of the unknown. I knew what was going to happen, so I could anticipate the next steps. I didn't want to be taking the next step, but I wasn't scared of it. Kyleigh had no idea what to expect. To her it was like taking a step in the dark. Being brave is easier when you can anticipate what is coming, but it is much harder to gather courage when you are faced with the unknown.

I spent the rest of the car ride explaining what was going to happen. I tried to relieve the tension and add some humor to get Kyleigh laughing. When we got to the Emergency Room, it did not take long to get us checked in and back to an exam room. The medical student came in first and spoke to Kyleigh and I to gather Kyleigh's medical history and perform an initial exam. I laughed later with Kyleigh because he told her how he was going to interview for an internship. When Kyleigh told him that I was in charge of the Transitional Internship, he became nervous and we never saw him again.

The Emergency Room attending physician came in and repeated the history and physical the student had obtained. He asked what kind of medicine I practiced, and I told him pediatric allergy/immunology. He then explained that yes, Kyleigh's blood sugar was very high (900mg/dL), but he wanted to get a chest x-ray to make sure it wasn't pneumonia.

Pneumonia?! What was he thinking? She didn't have a cough. She didn't have a fever. I needed to advocate for my child. She needed fluids and eventually insulin, but a chest x-ray was not necessary.

"Sir, I don't think a chest x-ray is necessary. Don't you think she has diabetes?" I politely asked to steer him away from the chest x-ray.

"Pneumonia can cause electrolyte shifts, so I think it is important to rule it out. Let me be the doctor," he replied.

I hate conflict. I needed courage in that moment, but I had none. Kyleigh needed an advocate, but I didn't have the strength to fill that role. I complied with the order for the chest x-ray and helped take Kyleigh to radiology. I knew the chest x-ray was not necessary, but I did it anyway, and then I proceeded to beat myself up about it. Kyleigh had received a lot of exposure to radiation throughout her short life due to follow-up cancer studies over the years. She did not need this x-ray.

Not surprisingly, the x-ray was normal. Was that x-ray the end of the world? No. Should I have held my ground better for my child? Absolutely. Kyleigh had no idea a chest x-ray was not an important part of the work-up for diabetes and could not speak up for herself about this frivolous part of her evaluation. I decided before we left the emergency room that night that I was going to be a better advocate for my child. I already learned from her cancer experience that a child with an illness needs a parent with courage to advocate for medical and school issues along with problems that arise in other areas of their life. I was going to be that advocate. There is only one diagnosis that gives patients a blood sugar of 900mg/dL and that's type 1 diabetes. Kyleigh was admitted to the pediatric ward that night for new onset type 1 diabetes—not pneumonia.

Learning Thoughts Of Courage Through My Patient

The need for courage from a parent who is caring for a child with chronic medical challenges became evident to me as I took care of my patients. The McElligatt family was amazing! I first met them in the clinic when I evaluated their pre-school aged adopted daughter for a diagnosis of eczema made by a dermatologist. I wasn't convinced of the diagnosis. Her eczema never looked like the typical eczema that I saw. I referred the child to another dermatologist, but the family and I remained skeptical of the dermatology assessment. Mrs. McElligatt was always apologetic for not trusting the opinion of the specialist. I appreciated the apologies, but I never felt like they were necessary because I, too, didn't agree with the specialist. This uncertainty with the diagnosis bonded us. We continued to treat the skin condition like eczema without ever really finding another diagnosis that was a better fit. It was easy to surmise early in our relationship that Mrs. McElligatt was an incredible parental advocate.

I really got to know the McElligatt family when they adopted a second daughter from Vietnam. Mrs. McElligatt spoke to me about the child before they headed to Vietnam because they knew the child had special needs. She had not received specific information on the concerns or expected treatment. She asked if I would be available to see the new baby when they returned to the United States after the adoption process was finalized in Vietnam. To be intimately involved in this incredible act of love was something that I considered a privilege of my role as a physician. Of course, I would be available!

When the day finally came, I was probably as excited to meet the new baby as the parents had been days earlier. The child was beautiful. She had been eating well since they picked her up from the orphanage, but she was a little underweight. I told them we would monitor her weight. I looked over her vaccine record and found several were missing. We created a plan to get her vaccines up to date. She was behind on her developmental milestones, and we would get her enrolled in early intervention services. All in all, things looked good.

I noticed, though, on physical exam that her eyes were not tracking together. It was subtle, but the child appeared to have strabismus (a lazy eye). I needed an ophthalmologist's opinion to confirm the diagnosis.

I gently explained my findings to the McElligatt's, and we developed a plan together. Vaccines, development, nutrition, and ophthalmology were all accounted for in our discussion. They would follow-up with me in the clinic in a month to check on the progress being made in these areas.

A month later, the child was back for a follow-up appointment. Again, I noticed her eye findings on physical exam and asked about the ophthalmology appointment. "They told us it was normal," Mrs. McElligatt explained. She went on the explain that the visit in ophthalmology was not what she anticipated and felt the exam was very cursory. I was suspicious but trusted the opinion of my colleagues. We agreed, though, that we would follow the recommendations of the eye doctors and "continue monitoring with follow-up in six months."

Shortly after this office visit, I bumped into the McElligatt's as they were taking care of other issues at the hospital. I stopped to chat briefly and saw the baby in the stroller. As I was admiring how much the infant had grown, I noticed the eyes were still not tracking together. I asked Mrs. McElligatt to tell me again when the child would be seen next in the ophthalmology clinic, and she told me it would be in 6–12 months. I became uncomfortable with the lengthy interval.

Similar to our past conversations about the older child's eczema, Mrs. McElligatt began her advocacy for the infant. She, too, noticed the eye finding. As we stood in the hospital hall, she told me about her discomfort with the previous ophthalmology visit. She had a nagging feeling that something wasn't right, and we needed to do something.

I listened to Mrs. McElligatt during this chance encounter. She was polite, courageous, and determined to get answers for her child. Her ability to advocate for the infant came from her deep love for this small human. As a mother of a chronically ill child, I was very familiar with this deep love that could rally a dose of courage for advocacy. I knew the importance of being heard, and I understood helplessness when fighting for your child. With her permission, I planned to reach out to the pediatric ophthalmologist and discuss my concerns. Mrs. McElligatt was grateful, and we parted ways.

The infant was seen again in the ophthalmology clinic soon after our discussion. That was the beginning of a long tumultuous journey treating congenital cataracts. Mrs. McElligatt's courage to speak up was instrumental in the care of her child, and her courageous ability to advocate for her children remains a skill that I will always admire about this loving mother.

Lessons On Courage

We avoid people, places, and events in our lives because of how we feel. I have avoided colleagues because I thought they didn't like the way I handled a situation. I have avoided returning to restaurants because I thought the service was slow and the food mediocre. I have avoided Christmas parties because I thought past attendees drank too much. My thoughts about each of these left me feeling uncomfortable and led to my avoidance.

Avoidance is our brain's way to keep us safe. It is a subconscious action in response to our thoughts and feelings. Sometimes we avoid because our brain remembers a past situation that created bad feelings. Our brain is protecting us from experiencing those feelings again. Sometimes we avoid because we are contemplating experiencing something new and our brain is again protecting us, but now it is trying to keep us safe by maintaining the status quo.

As a parent of a child with a medical problem, I found myself wanting to avoid doctor appointments. I understand now that my procrastination in scheduling appointments was the result of my thoughts. Those thoughts ultimately led to my feelings which is what I was really trying to avoid.

Some parents dread doctor appointments because the parent will be required to advocate for their child. When parents don't think they have the courage to advocate, they become fearful and avoid the doctors. I am a doctor, though, so this reason for avoidance seemed silly because I shouldn't be fearful of advocacy—but I was. Advocacy for your child involves agreeing, questioning, and perhaps disagreeing with a doctor, school official, or caretaker.

It can become difficult to create courage to advocate if we hold limiting beliefs. Limiting beliefs are thoughts we think over and over again until we believe them to be truths. They are anchored in our subconscious mind and limit us from acting. I held the belief that I am a people pleaser, so thoughts of disagreeing with someone—especially a colleague—created waves of fear. This left me paralyzed. These beliefs can disrupt our ability to feel courage.

While limiting beliefs keep us unmotivated, empowering beliefs can motivate us. Believing in yourself in your role as an advocate is a crucial step in the journey of growth. Courage through self-confidence becomes the cornerstone to empowerment, but this must start with the consciousness of your own thoughts.

Everyone can change the thoughts that are offered by their brain, but to successfully manage your mind requires choosing a thought you believe. For example, the thought of, *I will upset the ER physician,* was holding me back from advocating during Kyleigh's diabetes diagnosis. A better thought could have been, *I will help the physician do what's right for my child.* This latter thought will lead to the confidence and courage required for advocacy. Mrs. McElligatt always reminded me that she felt uncomfortable disagreeing with physicians, because she believed they knew more than her. I reminded her that she was the mother, and she always knew best. Practicing this thought allowed her to grow courage to advocate for her child's ophthalmology concerns.

The future of our child, regardless of the health issue, is never in our control. Sometimes it is expected that questions are left unanswered. We ask questions such as, "What's the next treatment?" or "What happens if this intervention doesn't work?" or "When will we be able to sleep through the night?" and we have no answers because of the unpredictability of chronic illnesses. As parents, living with uncertainty is uncomfortable, but it is a necessary part of life.

The twists and turns of a child's medical journey can sometimes be out of our control. We need to be cautious, though, that the known lack of control doesn't turn into defeat. I was recently discussing a classic psychology study by Dr. Seligman in which dogs were put in different circumstances and given an electric shock. The group of dogs who inferred that they did not have control of the shock, gave up, and didn't try to escape. The conversation about this study reminded me that as parents, we, too, can experience this behavior of learned helplessness. I could have easily become one of Seligman's dogs who gave up when things seemed out of my control.

Becoming defeated by uncertainty can destroy our courage and confidence. The job of advocacy is an important task when we are parenting a child with chronic needs. Advocacy can only be successfully accomplished with courage. If I allowed myself to be defeated by the unanswered questions of what was next in Kyleigh's neuroblastoma treatment, I would have stopped asking and lost my courage in advocating for Kyleigh in the physician's office. We know life is full of uncertainty, and a child's medical journey is not an exception. I worked to understand the underlying cause of my avoidance, and I practiced controlling my thoughts about advocacy to develop courage.

Advocacy for our child will, at times, require disagreements. We know what is best for our child as a parent, but not everyone will have the same opinion. The courage to face conflict is an important part of advocacy. Disagreements are important in many relationships we have throughout our life. Disagreements with a significant other, friends, or colleagues provides us with the ability to deepen a relationship, expand our thoughts, or discover new perspectives. We create shallow, superficial relationships when we impede the ability to debate thoughts.

Becoming comfortable with the feeling of discomfort can prevent resistance when needing to take a courageous step. When the limiting belief is, "I don't like disagreements," we generate fear leading us to avoid conflict. Changing the thought to, "I am fascinated by the opinions of others," can instead, generate a calm confidence to approach disagreements.

Speaking up and disagreeing or verbally expressing frustration takes courage. Courage is necessary when sharing a dissenting view or personal emotions because it creates vulnerability. We might be sharing thoughts that may trigger emotions from others and result in criticism. Being ready with the armor of courage allows us to effectively disagree.

Three rules to effectively disagree:

1. **BE FASCINATED.** Listen and try to understand why the person might believe what they believe. I could have been fascinated by asking the ER physician why he thought there was pneumonia despite the lack of respiratory symptoms. Mrs. McElligatt could have been fascinated by asking the ophthalmologist why he thought the child's eyes were normal. Don't miss the opportunity to understand why they believe what do.

2. **STAY ENGAGED.** Take a calm approach to continuing the conversation when you disagree. Using a phrase such as, "I want to understand your opinion, but I think I mine might be completely different." I could have calmly told the ER physician that my opinion of the concern for pneumonia was different than his, and I wanted him to continue so I could understand his opinion. Using this strategy would have also allowed Mrs. McElligatt to get further information from the ophthalmologist to better understand and calmly disagree.

3. **BE AWARE OF HOW YOU FEEL.** Physical signs can be caused by our thoughts. Is your pulse increasing? Are you feeling flushed? These symptoms remind you to be conscious of your own thinking and chose how to respond. I was annoyed with the ER physician and felt my heart pounding and blood rushing to my face. These signs could have been my reminder that my thought, *This doctor is a moron*, was not helpful. I can guess that Mrs. McElligatt experienced similar physical symptoms when trying to muster the courage for advocacy. We could have intentionally chosen the thought, *He is trying his best*, to create a sense of calm. This calmness doesn't mean we stop advocating, but it allows us to control our emotions before acting.

The goal of communicating is gaining an understanding of the other perspective. Our ability to be an advocate will not always be perfect. We will grow and evolve on this parenthood journey, and we will make mistakes. It becomes important to forgive ourselves when things don't go the way we intended. Use these times as opportunities to learn and maintain a positive mindset. Give yourself grace and encouragement.

Reaching any dream or aspiration requires courage despite the perceived risk and uncertainty. Advocacy is no different. The dreams and aspirations we have for ourselves are not at the forefront of our brain when we are parenting, but the goals we have for our child will require courageous advocacy to achieve.

Chapter 3

OVERWHELM

> *"Getting knocked down in life is a given. Getting up and moving forward is a choice." – Zig Ziglar*

O verwhelm is a feeling that comes from the flood of thoughts filling our brains. The brain can indulge in this feeling which, in turn, keeps us stuck and not moving forward in a productive way. The job of the brain is to keep us safe and maintain the status quo so when we are faced with a very new circumstance, the brain does not want to participate because there is risk to our safety. It becomes understandable that thoughts creating overwhelm keep us frozen and unable to take a step into the future. Our brains believe that inaction will keep us safe.

When children are diagnosed with medical issues, parents become overwhelmed with the needs of their child. As time goes by, the chaos of a disorganized life exacerbates their feelings and causes them to sink deeper into despair. Organization of their mind, time, and physical space becomes an important goal for combating the feelings of being overwhelmed. The parents who can move from despair to joy believe that they can acquire the skills to get their life in order.

Learning Thoughts Of Overwhelm Through Kyleigh

Shortly after receiving the diagnosis of neuroblastoma, I quickly learned something—parents with a chronically ill child become very good at lying. Any time we went to the hospital for an appointment or treatment, I was asked how I was doing. Each time I responded with, "I'm fine." This was a lie.

I was exhausted and the myriad of emotions seemed, at times, unbearable. My bedroom had transformed into a hospital room complete with IV poles containing feeding pumps.

It was no wonder I was tired because nighttime was terrible. Kyleigh wasn't eating—a side effect of chemo—but she needed nutrition. I was instructed by her doctors to do night feeds via a nasogastric (NG) tube. This meant that every night I placed a tube in her nose that reached her stomach. I taped the tube in place along her precious cheek. I attached the tube to a bag of formula and ran the tubing through the pump. I set the pump for a slow rate so she could easily digest it through the night. This became our bedtime routine followed by me rocking her until we both feel asleep in the chair. Kyleigh transformed from a happy, independent infant with rolls of baby fat to a clingy, terrified infant with saggy skin. I became a walking zombie who was going through the motions and preparing to crumble with the next hit.

I woke when Kyleigh stirred and gently placed her in her crib so I could lay down and get some needed rest. It wouldn't be long before I woke to the sound of a beeping pump. I walked to Kyleigh's crib to find the tube out of Kyleigh's nose, but still taped to her cheek and the mattress soaked with formula. She pulled out the tube in her sleep. After a few nights of this repeat interruption, I decided on another plan.

I learned from a pediatric attending physician that a good way to brush a toddler's teeth was to lay them on the floor with the child's arms spread wide. The parent's legs would be positioned over the child's arms pinning the shoulders so the child couldn't roll. The child's head would be braced between each of the parent's legs while the child's feet would be positioned by the parent's feet. This position allowed the parent to use both of their hands to brush the child's teeth without a concern for injuring the child with the toothbrush. I taught this position to many patients during their well child visits, but now I needed this position to keep my child safe during sleep.

Our bedtime routine soon transformed to include placing the NG tube, taping it in place, connecting the tubing, setting the pump, and now instead of rocking, we would lay in my bed in the "T" position. Kyleigh drifted in and out of sleep throughout the night. I attempted to sleep, but never fully relaxed since every little movement or sound made me open my eyes to check on things. My priority became Kyleigh's nutrition by making sure that nothing interrupted her feeds, even if I had to give up my own sleep.

Kyleigh's central line dressing changes were equally dramatic. I gathered all the supplies and placed them on the floor. I sat on the floor with Kyleigh again in the "T" position and began changing the dressing of the line that was coming out the top of her chest. The site needed to stay clean, since line infections were dangerous in a patient undergoing chemotherapy. As I worked on removing the old dressing, cleaning the area with my supplies, and replacing the dressing,

I sang, "Twinkle, Twinkle, Little Star." I knew Kyleigh would forever dislike this song since it became associated with something she hated, but I continued singing it over and over and over again. I tried to convince myself it helped make her calm but in reality, Kyleigh continued screaming and the song became a reminder that my experience of being a mother to a young infant was getting ripped away from me. I was the one who would forever dislike this song.

I took a leave of absence from my residency training to care for my daughter. Instead of entering the hospital every morning, I spent my day in the place that was once my home but now resembled a medical facility with pumps and shelves filled with supplies. Instead of rounds with patients, I placed NG tubes, cared for central lines, cleaned up the side effects of chemotherapy, and attended the doctor appointments and inpatient admissions. I was not fine.

I lived in a constant storm with the storm clouds filled with "overwhelm." This emotion rained down on me every day and I had no umbrella to protect me from the downpour. The feeling increased my fatigue and caused me to further ignore taking care of anyone except Kyleigh. I was not eating well. I was not exercising. I was not enjoying living my childhood dream of being a mom. It was a struggle. I thought that the constant lying about how I was doing would make the discomfort of being overwhelmed magically go away. I had often heard, "Fake it 'til you make it," but no matter how many times I said, "I'm fine," it wasn't changing the reality that I really wasn't ok.

Throughout the years, my feelings of overwhelm regarding Kyleigh ebbed and flowed. After she completed chemotherapy, I thought it was gone forever, but then it came roaring back every time she had a check-up to make sure her tumor was not recurring. I thought I had forgotten how to lie when Kyleigh was diagnosed with diabetes. My ability to lie about how "fine" I was reappeared without skipping a beat. I often wonder why it is so easy to say, "I'm fine." Perhaps it is the hope that if you keep saying it, you will actually be fine. Perhaps it is the desire to avoid burdening others with your world. Perhaps the truth is just too painful to share, so we don't. It doesn't matter the reason. Parents of chronically ill children are all very skilled at it. "I'm fine," is the mantra of the club.

Kyleigh was admitted to the pediatric ward after her diagnosis of type 1 diabetes. All the overwhelming emotions from years earlier came rushing back as I tried to sleep in the uncomfortable pull-out bed next to Kyleigh's hospital bed. The beeps of the pumps, the alarms of the vitals screens, and the frequent interruptions throughout the night put my mind back into the exhausted, overwhelmed state I struggled with previously. How was I ever going to manage this? I once again entered my zombie state of "fine."

The overwhelming emotions really flooded in the second day of Kyleigh's hospital admission. The goal of the admission was to decrease Kyleigh's extremely high blood sugar and to teach us the skills to be safe at home. I knew from my career as a pediatrician that caring for kids with a diagnosis of diabetes required supplies such as syringes, needles, glucose meters, strips, alcohol wipes, and so on. The hospital teaching needed to help us learn how to use all these supplies.

The endocrinology team came to Kyleigh's hospital room early in the morning. Kyleigh, with her cute smile and bed-head hairdo, reported that she was feeling great and was ready to leave. The doctors explained she couldn't be discharged until she understood some important things about her disease. They then turned to me and instructed me to go to the pharmacy and pick up the prescriptions that had been ordered. The team would be back later to demonstrate some of the supplies that I would pick up at the pharmacy.

I headed to the pharmacy after the team left to continue their rounds and see other patients. Kyleigh was relaxing with a movie so I knew she would be entertained in my absence. I walked the hallways of the hospital in the jeans and sweatshirt that had also served as my pajamas the previous night. I felt odd as I made my way to the pharmacy because my appearance was not consistent with my usual work attire. As I passed through the halls, I was in disbelief that once again we were cursed to be on the patient side of medicine.

I sat at the pharmacy waiting for the prescriptions to be filled and watched the individuals come and go from the pharmacy windows. Each patient had their own story and I tried to silently guess what diagnosis was bringing them to the pharmacy today. There was a mom with a toddler in a stroller who was fussy—ear infection. There was an older gentleman who knew the pharmacy process well—hypertension and hyperlipidemia. There was a middle-age woman with a rash on her arms—hives. Everyone seemed to walk away from the window with one or two pill bottles. My number was called, and I went to the window to receive two large grocery bags full of items. My heart raced as the sensation of nausea appeared. This was the emotion of overwhelm.

I grabbed the grocery bags and retraced the path I took earlier to get to the pharmacy. Now I felt even more out of place since I looked like I was hauling a load of food items from a grocery store down the halls of my hospital. I dreaded each step thinking that I was going to bump into a colleague.

I wasn't ready to see anyone yet, especially not looking like a grocery delivery person. I finally got to Kyleigh's room.

As I walked into the room, Kyleigh was lying in bed with Archie. Archie was beautiful German shepherd who was one of the therapy dogs that visited patients at the hospital. This was such a strange moment filled with irony because only a month earlier, Kyleigh completed a service project in which she volunteered her time to create a beautiful scrapbook filled with different photos of Archie visiting patients throughout the hospital. Who could have predicted that the creator of the scrapbook would now be one of the patients that Archie visited? I quickly snapped a photo knowing that Kyleigh's new diagnosis would be awarded a place in Archie's scrapbook. As I looked through the camera lens, I felt like I was looking at someone else's life. It felt strange to be witnessing the poignant meeting of these two creatures. A deep sadness came over me when I realized that they were previously connected through a service project, but now their connection was because Kyleigh was a patient.

After we visited with the trainer and Archie, they went off to visit other patients and we were left with the grocery bags. Kyleigh was excited to figure out what was in the bags. She asked me to unload them on the bed. I grabbed the first bag and dumped it on the foot of the bed followed by the second bag. Kyleigh started picking up the items and asking questions about each one. I stood staring, silent, and felt the wave of emotions that hit me like a tsunami. Our new life was represented in the pile of supplies at the foot of a hospital bed. In that moment, I was absolutely overwhelmed.

Words wouldn't form to respond to Kyleigh's questions and I continued standing frozen in front of this mess on the bed. After feeling like the world had stopped for an eternity, I started organizing the supplies. Short-acting insulin in one pile, long-acting insulin in another, glucagon and glucose tablets in a third, and so on. Some may have thought I was busily sorting to ignore our new life, but I was really dealing with overwhelm the only way I knew how—getting organized.

▌Learning Thoughts Of Overwhelm Through My Patient

I have cared for countless children both as a pediatrician and as an allergist/immunologist and truly loved each one of my patients, even if I just saw them once for a brief office visit. There were some patients, though, that found a permanent residence in my heart. My experience with Kyleigh allowed me to understand how overwhelming it could be to care for a child with a chronic illness. The supplies, the physician appointments, the school appointments, the medicine, and the side effects of the medicine created a stressful experience.

Megan was one of my patients who would permanently occupy my heart. She was a beautiful girl with significant developmental delays. She wore glasses and had a tough time carrying on a conversation, but as a physician, I was privileged to care for her. She had seizures and scoliosis, among other health problems.

Megan was seen by numerous subspecialty physicians, and each documented the medical visit in a paper chart. She was sent to several different hospitals and each physician wrote their own piece to Megan's story. Usually, a paper chart is filled with about an inch worth of doctor's notes, but Megan's chart was several inches thick. Her medical chart was not only huge but also disorganized, which led to unproductive medical appointments with subspecialists because they repeated information that was already known.

Megan's mother was an amazing woman. Megan was one of three children in the family, and each was incredibly loved, but Megan required the constant attention. Megan's mom came to the appointments pushing Megan in a medical stroller, and we discussed any new medical issues with Megan or caught up on recent subspecialty appointments Megan had completed. We also spent a few minutes talking about life and the challenges with caring for Megan. We shared in our unified frustration of not having a name for the syndrome we believed Megan had. I knew being able to diagnose the specific syndrome would allow me to provide better preventive medical care. Megan's mom knew a syndrome would allow her to have knowledge about the future. This shared frustration and common understanding of being overwhelmed was the foundation of a friendship.

Megan's medical problems placed a tremendous amount on the plate of Megan's mom, but it never seemed to phase her, even though I knew it did. Despite the challenges with Megan, her mom stayed focused on working to find the name of a syndrome that explained all of Megan's health problems. I, too, was convinced that there was a diagnosis of a syndrome that was not yet revealed for Megan.

One day I learned Megan was accepted for an evaluation at National Institute of Health. We knew this appointment might be the key to figuring out the underlying reason for all Megan's health issues. I was empathetic to the family's emotion of overwhelm, so I reached out to Megan's mom and instructed her to bring Megan's medical records to my office during my administrative time. She arrived in my office that afternoon, and we took apart Megan's huge, disorganized record. We sat in my office and started putting every clinical note into piles by specialty: Allergy/Immunology, Cardiology, Dermatology, Developmental, Ophthalmology,

Orthopaedics, and so on. Well past the closing time of clinic, Megan's mom and I sat in my office surrounded by piles of papers.

I sent Megan's mom home before it got too late and told her I would finish the project. I grabbed binders and dividers and began hole punching the piles and assembling the newly organized medical binders. I delivered the binders to Megan's house the following day to be certain that they would be available for the upcoming NIH appointment. The relief that appeared on Megan's mom's face when I showed her the finish product was a gift. We had just tackled overwhelm by getting organized. This would allow Megan's mom to keep taking steps toward the goal of a diagnosis. Megan's mom and I did ultimately accomplish our goal—she was diagnosed with Kleefstra Syndrome.

Lessons On Overwhelm

Having a child with a chronic condition will naturally lead to being overwhelmed. Overwhelmed with caring for your child. Overwhelmed with the need to advocate or ask for help. Overwhelmed with creating balance in your life. Experiencing overwhelm is normal, but we become stuck when we continue carrying this emotion.

Feeling negative emotions like overwhelm or worry is part of living, but continuing to live with the emotion is a choice. When my daughter was diagnosed with diabetes, I stared at all her supplies and immediately felt overwhelmed. As life continued, I continued feeling this emotion and despite having a long to-do list, I would find myself binging on television. I was not motivated. I didn't realize at the time, motivation is something we create, not something that is bestowed upon us.

Understanding the connection between our mind and our actions reveals my lack of motivation was because I was overwhelmed. I was trying to escape my feeling of being overwhelmed and instead sought pleasure doing brainless activities and waiting for motivation to appear. As this behavior continued, my to-do list grew longer, and I became even more overwhelmed. I was in a never-ending cycle.

We can choose how we think and as a result, we choose how we feel. I didn't want to feel overwhelmed, so I began practicing techniques to change how I was thinking. I learned that the brain tries to protect and when we are trying to change, the mind resists because the status quo is safe. It was time to take control of my new life and build confidence in myself that I could stay balanced in my roles as a mother and career woman.

Changing thoughts leading to indulgent emotions takes practice. It is similar to a person faced with entering a pool. They don't want to do it initially because they are afraid it is cold. As the person dips their toes in, they provide evidence to their brain that the water is comfortable. Slowly, but surely, the person enters the water. Our thoughts about a motivated life take time to change, but continuing to provide evidence to your brain allows the overwhelm to slowly resolve.

When parenting a child with a medical problem, there is no benefit to becoming stressed and overwhelmed. These are normal emotions, but the lack of action we create from these emotions will not help move us forward. Feeling overwhelmed would not cure Kyleigh's cancer. Feeling overwhelmed would not make type 1 diabetes go away. Feeling overwhelmed would not make Megan's health issue go away. The emotion of overwhelm is not useful. Changing thoughts, though, allows the brain to become unstuck.

Feeling overwhelmed is an uncomfortable emotion. If you pause and pay attention to the changes you notice in your body when you are overwhelmed, you may notice your pulse might increase or a lump might form in the back of your throat. There might be a pit in the bottom of your stomach and your head might feel heavy. Physical signs and symptoms can be a result of the emotions we have. These physical findings can force us to pay attention to our emotional state.

It is overwhelming to be a parent of a sick child. We think our role as a parent instead has been changed to a 24/7 nurse who doesn't take breaks. The good news is that our thoughts and therefore, feelings are optional. We have the option to choose another thought which can create a different emotion, but this requires awareness and practice.

As the mother of a cancer patient, I became overwhelmed with the NG tubes, central lines, and countless admissions and doctor appointments. I was overwhelmed because my thought was, *I can't manage all of this.* When we dwell on this specific thought, it will of course, create an emotion of overwhelm. I realized it was not the medical supplies or appointments that made me overwhelmed, but rather my thoughts about all the things I needed to do as a mother of a chronically ill child.

The thoughts that create the emotion of overwhelm can be categorized into four categories.

1. ALL OR NOTHING THOUGHTS. Our brain is focused on all the medical issues and appointments and makes us think we can't manage. If we can't handle everything, we can't handle any of it. This is common thinking that leads to the emotion of overwhelm in parents with chronically ill children.

Refocusing our brain on the appointment next week, not the multiple appointments this year, can help dispel the overwhelming feeling.

2. PERFECTIONIST THOUGHTS. My ultimate goal was to allow Kyleigh to live a long, heathy, prosperous life. On some days, though, her blood sugars were too high or too low and I focused on what I did to cause the problem. I became overwhelmed by thinking I needed to be a perfect mom of a diabetic child, helping maintain blood sugars in range at all times. I wanted to give up doing anything to help, since my brain continued to loop the erroneous thinking that the one day of bad sugars would inevitably mean her long life was not obtainable. The end goal seemed unobtainable and made me overwhelmed. My emotion of overwhelm did not fuel motivation, but rather resulted in inaction.

3. "SHOULD" THOUGHTS. *I should be able to handle a chemo kid and a toddler*, was a thought that swirled in my head and left me expecting I could be a superhuman parent. Instead, it promoted a sense of overwhelm. "Should" thoughts create expectations that lead to being overwhelmed because we have thoughts about not meeting the expectations.

4. PEOPLE PLEASING THOUGHTS. As a parent, I was overwhelmed by Kyleigh's nighttime feeds that required the NG tube. This came from the idea that Kyleigh's physicians thought this daily ritual was something easy to do. It was overwhelming because

these physicians were my colleagues and teachers, and I did not want to disappoint them. Overwhelm was the result of thoughts of not meeting these expectations.

I used to have trouble trying to picture what my life would look like in the future because all the overwhelming thoughts were consuming my brain. If I sat in a quiet place and closed my eyes to envision life, I just saw darkness. My brain then started drifting to all the thoughts that were creating that darkness—Kyleigh's appointments, medication refills, and school meetings. The darkness quickly turned into incessant overwhelming thoughts about the health of my child.

I didn't want to live in a constant state of being overwhelmed, so attempting to dig myself out of these emotions, I decided to attend a personal growth conference. During the conference, we were asked to close our eyes and imagine our future. The speaker asked questions as the audience had their eyes closed: What does your future house look like? What does your future neighborhood look like? What is your future-self wearing? And on and on.

I sat in the audience with my eyes closed hoping that this would be the time I could vividly see how I wanted my life. I had paid money to attend the conference, so this time it had to work. Sadly, all I saw was darkness. After the list of questions, the speaker then told everyone to open their eyes and spend the next ten minutes writing in detail everything they saw. I opened my eyes and at the top of my paper I wrote the word, "Nothing." For ten minutes, I stared at a full sheet of paper with seven letters written at the top. That was the moment I committed to doing the work to begin dreaming again.

Dreaming about the future can bring hope, excitement, and motivation. Our focus on the future keeps us moving forward. We would never expect a runner to run a new trail with their eyes closed or looking backward. We would expect them to stay focused on the path ahead, moving quickly, and staying out of danger. But I was trying to navigate the trail of life with my eyes closed.

Managing thoughts and emotions helps us dream. My eyes were closed because I was wallowing in emotions created from thoughts about being the parent of a chronically ill child. As I worked on the thoughts my brain was telling me and changed how I was feeling, I started thinking about the future. At first, like an occasional black and white TV show, the thoughts were not frequent or vivid. The vivid movie reels come when you begin to choose what you think and how you feel.

Dreaming for a young child is easy. Their imagination about the future is extraordinary at times. We were once like this, but somewhere along the way, we became consumed with the overwhelming part of life. We became stuck and stopped looking ahead. It is never too late to revisit that childhood imagination and once again learn to focus on the future. It may feel safer to keep your eyes closed, but in reality, we are alive and well when our eyes are open and we are choosing our journey.

Chapter 4

SUPPORT

> *"Try to be a rainbow in someone's cloud."*
> *– Maya Angelou*

I used to believe the universe only gives us what we can handle. I realize now this was a limiting belief that caused me to be challenged when I needed to ask for help. During times of crisis, I found myself shying away from reaching out to others for support, because I was afraid it was a sign of weakness. I didn't want to ask anyone for help watching Jake while I was caring for Kyleigh. I didn't want to ask for help at work covering patients when I needed to be at an appointment. I was creating fear by having thoughts that asking for help meant I was not capable. Asking for help can be a challenging action in many areas of our lives, but especially when parenting. Our brain suggests thoughts that we should be able to do everything. If we can't accomplish everything, we are left with feelings of guilt. Fear was also created by having thoughts that assistance would make me a burden, and I would be imposing on others.

Learning Thoughts Of Support Through Kyleigh

When Kyleigh was diagnosed with neuroblastoma, my world fell apart. I wanted to run away from the bad dream happening before me. My energy was consumed by caring for my daughter and worrying about the future. Trying to get out of the bed in the morning became something I needed to do rather than want to do. All my other tasks such as cooking, cleaning, and parenting my two-year-old son were placed on the back burner.

I was familiar with the saying, "It takes a village," when referring to raising a child. I can absolutely say this statement is even more applicable to parenting when a child with medical needs is involved. I didn't have the strength or time to do anything other than care for Kyleigh. I had lots of colleagues and friends offer to help and said to let them know "if I needed anything." I never had the strength, though, to reach out for help because I was too busy working to make everyone believe I was fine.

One day while Kyleigh was an inpatient, I stepped out of her room to go grab a bite to eat. When I reappeared, there was a large basket in the room with a note. The note said it was from a fellow resident, and the basket was filled with a lasagna family dinner to include salad and dessert. Instructions were in the basket on ingredients and cooking times. The sender thought of every detail including a tablecloth, plates, silverware, serving spoon, salad tongs and dressing. This display of support brought tears to my eyes and could not have been more perfect.

The next day while rocking Kyleigh, another fellow resident appeared with a box. In the box was another meal, carefully packaged with all the attention to detail that the first basket demonstrated. It was definitely a labor of love, and I was appreciative. The resident who delivered the box explained that several residents organized a "meal train," knowing that I might need some help while Kyleigh was undergoing treatment. The meal train lasted for a week or two, but with freezing some meals and leftovers, we were fed well.

Our friends and fellow residents showed up for us during this time, but they weren't the only ones. I was fortunate to have my mother-in-law help care for Jake and household tasks. I was grateful for family that visited and lent a hand. It absolutely takes a village.

Gestures of physical support were appreciated during this challenging time. Just knowing that someone was there for us made all the difference in the world. Leaning on others during tough times is not a sign of weakness, but rather a sign of courage. I witnessed that physical support such as giving a hug, holding a hand, or making a meal can be an incredibly powerful way to show someone that you care.

Eventually, I knew Kyleigh needed to learn to care for and support herself, too. It is difficult to parent a child with a chronic illness because you want the child to feel supported, but you don't want to create a "vulnerable" child—a child who doesn't develop resiliency. Kyleigh tried to be a "normal" child and not draw attention to her diabetes, and I tried to parent Kyleigh just like I would parent a "normal" child. Her diagnosis of diabetes, though, was part of our lives and this was not changing any time soon.

I didn't coddle Kyleigh. I didn't lower my expectations for her because she had diabetes. I encouraged her independence, just like I did with my other kids. Kyleigh's siblings caught on to my style of parenting—concern without hovering, along with normalizing her disease. Jake and Kyleigh were only about eighteen months apart in age, so they sometimes told people they were twins. Kyleigh skipped the sixth grade, so they were both the same grade level academically. During eighth grade, they attended a teen social event together. Kyleigh had her diabetes supplies with her, including her insulin pump device stuck to her upper arm when they headed out the door. Both the kids were excited for the event.

When I picked up the kids, I was excited to hear about the event and the kids were full of life when they hopped into the car. I initially got the usual, "It was fun," brief responses from them, but with some additional questioning, I started hearing some details about kids they met, games they played, and food they ate. After several minutes of talking, Kyleigh said, "Mom! I need to tell you a story."

She explained that some of the kids didn't know anything about diabetes and were surprised to see the pump on her arm. They watched her prick her finger before she ate any of the food and then continued to observe as she programmed the pump to deliver her insulin dose. Kyleigh said she felt embarrassed because she knew the children were staring and chatting about the insulin pump, but she tried to ignore it and not let it bother her.

Kyleigh's story continued as she recounted that one child came up to Jake and asked, "What's that thing on your sister's arm?" Jake, without skipping a beat said, "She's trying to cut back." The child looked at him with a strange expression of confusion. Jake put his two fingers together and brought them to his lips imitating a person smoking a cigarette.

Throughout the event, it became the joke that Kyleigh's insulin pump was a nicotine patch so my thirteen-year-old daughter could "cut back" on her smoking. I looked in the rear-view mirror when Kyleigh finished the story with a grin and caught her high-fiving Jake for his quick wit.

As a parent of a diabetic child, my initial thought was "Rats! We missed an opportunity to educate kids on type 1 diabetes," but I then quickly realized there would be plenty of opportunities in the future to educate children. I decided instead to savor this moment as I witnessed Kyleigh's excitement about Jake's gift of humor. His humor helped to lighten the mood and was a tremendous display of support for his sibling. The value of this incident was priceless. Kyleigh's initial feeling of awkwardness for being different faded away when her brother supported her and was quickly replaced with confidence allowing her to enjoy the event and walk away with new friends.

The support Kyleigh felt from her siblings was very important, and I highlighted those moments to make sure that she knew her family had her back. The support from her friends was equally important, especially while trying to manage the trials and tribulations of adolescence with a little diabetes sprinkled on top. When Kyleigh transferred to a new high school at the start of her junior year, one of these friends was Joe. Joe was kind and made Kyleigh feel welcome in this new school environment.

One day, Kyleigh was walking with Joe when she reached into her diabetes supply bag, and trash fell out. Joe asked what it was. Kyleigh explained that it was an old insulin pump pod. These pods would get filled with insulin and replaced on Kyleigh's arm every third day after they had delivered the medication. Kyleigh and Joe chatted more about diabetes and Kyleigh explained that November was

Diabetes Awareness Month. When the conversation ended, Joe asked if he could have the old pod. Kyleigh looked a bit puzzled but gave it to him.

Joe went home that night and glued the pod on a black band. The next day at school, Joe showed up with the black band tied around his arm. All day people asked what it was. Joe explained, "It's an insulin pump. My friend, Kyleigh, has to wear one so I am wearing one to show her that I support her, and because it is Diabetes Awareness Month!" Kyleigh and Joe took a photo together at school that day proudly displaying their insulin pods. She texted me the picture, and I cried when Kyleigh told me this story. She couldn't stop telling me how thankful she was for people like Joe. She was beaming with gratitude. Kyleigh grew a little taller that day because she stood up straight with confidence.

I wanted to shout Joe's wonderful display of support from the rooftops. I, too, was grateful to Joe and after asking if I could use their picture, I posted it on a Facebook group and even sent it to the Ellen DeGeneres show. Kyleigh and Joe never got an invitation to the Ellen show, but they were content with the "likes" and "comments" on the Facebook post.

I am grateful for these signs of support and know these are the moments I need to recognize and encourage. Kyleigh struggled with being the kid who was "different" because of her chronic illness. The kindness and support of Jake and Joe was tremendously valuable and helped teach many of their peers that difference is what makes this world beautiful.

Learning Thoughts Of Support Through My Patient

I knew firsthand about the challenges of life with a chronically ill child. Your priorities shift, and life becomes a juggling act. It is hard, really hard, to accomplish all things. As a physician, there were times I noticed during an office visit that a parent was looking a little disheveled or was missing the necessary school form, but the child was well kept. I always knew this meant that while they were juggling for their child, their own balls were being dropped despite every attempt to keep them all in the air.

Kate O'Leary's mother was definitely a juggler. Kate was a school-aged child of a physician colleague. She was one of five kids and the diagnosis of type 1 diabetes hit their family like a ton of bricks. They adjusted the best they could to their new life of finger sticks and insulin dosing. As a pediatrician, I periodically saw the family to make sure that Kate's blood sugar was doing well.

One day, Mrs. O'Leary brought Kate in to see me with siblings in tow. She appeared a little frazzled in my office and at first, I couldn't figure out if it was because Mrs. O'Leary was having trouble with Kate's diabetes, or if she was just busy being a mom to lots of kids. I asked how things were going and realized that her problem was both—also, Kate's dad was in the military and he had recently deployed. Mrs. O'Leary was left managing the household as a solo parent which is a challenge for any parent, but it becomes a heavier burden when you're the parent of a child with medical needs.

During the visit, Mrs. O'Leary explained that her biggest hurdle was preparing meals for the family. She had given up trying to prepare meals for herself, but she continued to struggle to have nutritious meals ready for the children. She was very concerned because she knew the importance of nutrition when trying to manage diabetes. Kate's blood sugars had been all over the place because of the fly-by-the-seat-of-your-pants food options. I listened as she explained the craziness of her life. Her days were filled with taking the kids to school, helping them with homework, transporting them to activities, potty-training a toddler, and changing diapers of an infant. There was really no time to pause and cook a meal.

"Let me help," I said, but Mrs. O'Leary was not going to let her pediatrician step in to assist. She declined my offer of assistance, but I realized that a general offer to lend a hand is sometimes too much to even think about when struggling with life's tasks. I recognized Mrs. O'Leary's resistance to my offer. Just as I was in the past, Mrs. O'Leary was "fine," but this lie was hiding the exhaustion. I knew how exhausted she was feeling, and I could guess that there wasn't energy to even think of ways that someone could help. I decided I needed a more specific offer so Mrs. O'Leary didn't have to think.

I restated my offered, "I will bring you meals." Mrs. O'Leary looked at me with a puzzled expression on her face. "I can't have you do that," she said. I explained to her that I knew of a place to assemble nutritious family meals that could be frozen, but easily defrosted and cooked on the desired day. This would make it easy to prepare meals and eliminate lengthy trips to the grocery store. My offer wasn't really a question, but rather a statement of what I was going to do regardless of any resistance I encountered.

"You would do that?" Mrs. O'Leary asked.

"I am going to do that. Do the kids have any food dislikes that I should avoid?" I asked.

During the office visit, Mrs. O'Leary agreed to my offer to bring meals and we arranged the date based on the opportunity in my schedule to assemble the meals. She was surprised, yet very grateful because she knew this support would help make life a little easier. She left my office with a smile after giving me her address, and the kids were excited I was coming to visit.

A few days later, I brought a cooler to the food assembly store and worked for the next few hours assembling meals for Kate's family. After assembling each meal, I placed the meal bag in the cooler and confidently knew each meal could take a little bit of burden off Mrs. O'Leary's plate, just like the meal train had for me years earlier. I finished at the store, paid for the thirty meals I made, left the store, and loaded the cooler into my car to head to Kate's house.

The meal delivery was priceless. It was late evening when I arrived, and I knocked on the door with my cooler. The house was quiet when I entered, and Mrs. O'Leary looked shocked to see me. Even though she knew I was coming, I think she doubted I would carry out my offer. Mrs. O'Leary and I unloaded the contents of the cooler into the freezer, and I explained how each bag had a sticker with cooking instructions. She was excited to have this gift, which was really giving her the gift of time.

After we finished, Mrs. O'Leary asked if I would mind saying hello to the kids. She explained that they were lying in bed waiting for me, and she knew the knock at the door stirred their excitement. "Of course!" I exclaimed. I followed her up the stairs to Kate's room. Kate was sitting in bed with a book, grinning from ear to ear. She gave a quick glance to her mother, as if silently asking permission to get out of bed, but without waiting for a response, Kate leaped out of bed and came running toward me for a hug.

I spent a few minutes reading to Kate, and then I said quickly said good night to her siblings. I left their house that evening with a full heart. I loved being able to help. On the drive home I reflected on my evening. Through this experience, I learned that if I need help in the future and find myself hesitating to ask for assistance, I need to remind myself of this warm feeling. This feeling would be a gift I could give someone by allowing them to help me. Maybe this belief could remove my hesitation to ask for help.

Lessons On Support

Asking for help is a sign of strength, confidence, and resourcefulness. It shows that you are willing to admit when you need assistance, and that you are not afraid to ask for it. You aren't weak when you ask for help, but rather weakness is not asking for help when you need it. I was struggling when Kyleigh was diagnosed with neuroblastoma and believed I could do everything: be a caretaker to my sick child, be a caretaker to my healthy toddler, be a resident, and be a spouse. I needed help juggling all the tasks involved in these roles of my life during this stressful time. Assistance does not make you a burden, it makes you human. This sign of humanness can make you more approachable in the future.

Over time, I questioned my original thought that the universe only gives us only what we can handle. I realized that a better belief is that there are times in our lives when we are given too much. During these times, the universe is teaching us how to ask for help or teaching us how to be grateful for support.

Don't be afraid to take the step and reach out to others. More often than not, people will be happy to help you and you will help them feel validated just like I was when I was able to help Mrs. O'Leary. People feel pride when someone views them as an individual who can provide a solution to a problem. Asking for help gives others an opportunity to shine and share their gifts. We are not imposing or burdening others.

Four ways to improve supporting each other:

1. **AWARENESS.** Recognize you need help and ask for it. This involves setting aside the thoughts causing us to be resistant to this step. Asking for help takes courage because we all want to be superheroes and be able to accomplish everything, but this is not humanly possible. As parents of children with medical needs, we know firsthand how challenging it is to ask for help. I couldn't be at work seeing patients at the same time I was on the inpatient ward with Kyleigh during her chemotherapy sessions. I courageously asked for a leave of absence from my training to focus on my daughter's healthcare needs. Colleagues would need to cover my patients, but I was stretched too thin. Obtaining assistance is worth experiencing the transient discomfort that we might experience when asking for help.

2. **CELEBRATE.** Celebrate the support of others when you witness it. Celebrating others can be done with kind words or a quick note. It provides an opportunity for our mind to focus on gratitude. Shortly after my visit to the O'Leary's house, a letter came to me in the clinic. In it was a note of thanks from Mrs. O'Leary and a beautiful picture drawn

by Kate. That picture still hangs in my office as a reminder of celebrating kindness.

Providing positive reinforcement for acts of support will encourage the individual to repeat the behavior in the future. Science has taught us that behavior that is positively reinforced is repeated. Displays of appreciation and celebration of simple acts of kindness have the ability to compound kindness throughout our world.

3. **ASSIST OTHERS.** Be someone to offer support and model how you want others to show up. We should provide support when we know it is needed rather than wait to be called upon to assist. We understand the challenges involved in asking for help and should use empathy to assist before we are asked. We have heard well-intentioned individuals tell us to let them know when we need "something." We know what other parents need when we have previously walked in their shoes. Be specific with the ways you can help such as making meals, providing cleaning support, or babysitting. Don't take, "No," as an answer. My colleagues understood this when Kyleigh was diagnosed with neuroblastoma. The meals quietly appearing before I asked was greatly appreciated.

4. **CREATE A VILLAGE.** Surround yourself with people you trust. We cannot know everything. Successful people have learned to create a "village" of trustworthy people. Surrounding yourself with

people who can help you in different situations is highly valuable. Kyleigh had Jake and Joe as her village. They were trustworthy supporters who she knew would be an emotional post to lean on.

Emotions

Chapter 5

FEAR

> *"You gain strength, courage, and confidence by every experience in which you really stop to look fear in the face. You must do the thing which you think you cannot do."*
> *— Eleanor Roosevelt*

Fear is an unpleasant, often strong emotion caused by anticipation or awareness of danger. All living creatures can experience this emotion to stay alive and remain safe, but what makes us unique as humans is that we have the freedom of choosing how to cope with it. While fear for immediate danger is useful and necessary, humans have developed unnecessary fears about potential dangers that may or may not happen in the future. This is rarely helpful and can act as a barrier preventing us from courageously acting.

You cannot live a full life without the emotion of fear. We experience fear in all aspects of our lives—relationships, career, personal health, and especially our role as parents. The brain's job is to keep us safe. When we are faced with a risky situation, the mind creates thoughts leading to fear. The thoughts might even be about things that have not occurred because the mind wants to avoid future discomfort. It doesn't always mean there is imminent danger.

Learning Emotion Of Fear Through Kyleigh

Kyleigh was still admitted to the pediatric ward when my village was helping with a meal train. Kyleigh's doctors originally thought her neuroblastoma was well-contained and she would only require surgical intervention. After her initial surgery, they explained her stage of neuroblastoma was more serious and would require chemotherapy, but there was one more step that needed to occur to be able to fully draft Kyleigh's treatment plan. Kyleigh needed a test to see if an oncogene (cancer gene) called c-myc was amplified in her tumor. If this test came back positive, she would need a bone marrow transplant.

I had never cared for a child during a bone marrow transplant, since that was not a procedure done at our hospital. I cared for children who were receiving chemotherapy on many occasions, and I understood the chemotherapy process and risks of this treatment. I knew a patient's blood counts could drop and sometimes the counts were low enough to require transfusions. I knew chemotherapy could give children mouth sores and a poor appetite that could lead to difficulty gaining weight. I knew receiving chemotherapy meant the child had an increased risk of infections, so family members needed to be cautious about visiting. Even knowing all of this, I also knew that kids were resilient, and the side effects of chemotherapy could be overcome. Transplants, however, had all the risks of chemotherapy plus more such as graft versus host disease (donor cells attack the patient's body cells). Since I had no experience in transplant care, I was scared of the transplant process that I had only read about. Everything the textbooks taught me about transplants was frightening.

Kyleigh remained in the hospital while we were awaiting the results of the oncogene test. My thoughts swirled around everything a transplant could bring. I feared transferring hospitals and being under the care of doctors who were not my colleagues. This would require placing my trust in strangers and hoping they would treat us like we were one of them. I feared trying to find a donor. I knew this could be a complicated feat and I thought about what would happen if we couldn't find a donor. I feared losing my daughter.

In the days awaiting results, I cried as I held Kyleigh and visited the hospital chapel, praying for good news. I was consumed with fear and attempted to tell myself, "Everything will be fine," but not really believing my own words.

I stared at Kyleigh as she slept with her thumb in her mouth and wondered if this was a result of not knowing what else to do, or if my gaze was still because I needed to soak in every precious moment before the universe made things worse. It was in these moments that I realized I was powerless and had no control of her future, but I could be present with her. I sat in the stillness filled with fear. The fear was so great at times that it felt like it was physically crushing me. It was all-consuming and took over every thought. Even when I wasn't actively thinking about it, the fear was always with me. It would hit me in waves throughout the day and suddenly wash over me out of nowhere.

My whole body would tense up with fear and I would shake. I felt like I couldn't breathe, and my heart raced. Fear became debilitating and made it hard to focus on anything else. It added to my physical and mental exhaustion and followed me like a shadow.

Thankfully, the test results came back and we found out that Kyleigh did not have the amplified oncogene. We were relieved, but my fear didn't immediately go away. I still felt fear inside me even though the immediate threat was gone. My body and soul had been on high alert for the past several days, and it took time before I once again felt safe. The feeling of hope kept me grounded and focused on being able to process my fear.

It is amazing how much power fear had over me. It took control of my thoughts and my actions, leaving me feeling helpless. I will never forget how fear took over my life, but maintaining hope and processing fear creates the ability to come out the other side.

Even after that, fear was still present in my life. Kyleigh was twenty years old when she moved into a cute little house in a beautiful community in New Jersey. Kyleigh had lived with diabetes for many years before moving to pursue her dreams of medical school. She was proud of her autonomy, and I was proud of the independent woman she was becoming. Kyleigh's diabetic alert dog was also happy in her new home.

I was excited for her, but very nervous because this would be the first time that she would be living by herself. She always had a roommate in the past and this gave me comfort that I had someone to reach out to if Kyleigh's blood sugars were dangerously high or low. This time was going to be different because I wasn't going to have a safety net, but Kyleigh would have her dog.

My phone has an app that is connected to Kyleigh's continuous glucose monitor, and it alarms if her measurements are too high or too low. We have a deal. If her blood sugar needs to be fixed, she will send me a quick text such as "fixing." If I don't hear from her and a few alarms go by, I reach out to her to ask "fixing?" If there is still no response, I call. This has been our virtual dance for years. She has always answered the phone, but it was comforting to have the contact information of a roommate just in case of emergencies. The move to New Jersey would mean no "ICE" roommates, but I never needed them so I was confident all would be fine.

Kyleigh's periodically wacky blood sugars did not suddenly change when she moved to New Jersey, but we maintained our virtual dance and understood what part in the dance we each had. It wasn't unusual when my phone started alarming due to her CGM readings in the middle of the night. Just like I had done in the past, I waited in a half-asleep state in bed. My phone alarmed again. Still half-asleep, I looked at the CGM app and saw "48." I couldn't wait much longer for Kyleigh to text because this was low, so I sent her a "fixing?" message. I laid in bed and waited. The alarm went off again, but no text from Kyleigh. I picked up my phone and called her. Voicemail. I called again. Again voicemail. The CGM alarm kept going off periodically to remind me of the danger I was trying to avoid.

Now I was awake, and my heart was beating a little faster when my brain started telling me, *Kyleigh always answers her phone.* I sat up in bed and called again. Voicemail. I then tried using FaceTime realizing that the FaceTime ring is different than the regular ring of the phone. Still no answer. I texted her with a simple, "Hello?" but no response. Now my mind began to race as fast as my heart. This was a new part of our virtual dance that we entered without practicing our dance moves. Now what? I needed to think fast because I knew the dangers of a low sugar number. When blood sugar is low, a person's cells are not getting fuel. Brain cells don't have the ability to function, so a diabetic can go into a coma and die. Worry was becoming fear. Fear was rapidly escalating to terror.

I decided to call Alec, Kyleigh's boyfriend. Alec was a Marine stationed in California. He needed to know I was concerned. I thought maybe he could help me brainstorm what my next step should be. Alec answered, but I could hear that I startled him from sleep. "Alec, Kyleigh's blood sugar is really low, and I can't get a hold of her. Do you have a phone number for Kate, Kyleigh's neighbor? Maybe she could go bang on Kyleigh's door," I said. He had a number and decided to call Kate while I kept trying the phone. We promised to keep each other posted as to whomever we were able to reach, Alec with Kate or me with Kyleigh. We hung up and I was now out of bed and standing with my room light on. I kept FaceTiming while my app kept alarming. A minute or two later, Alec called back. He couldn't get a hold of Kate, so I told him I was calling the police while he took over calling Kyleigh.

I searched for the police number, called, and explained the situation. They said they could send an officer over, but after I gave them Kyleigh's address, I was told I called the wrong police department. I was ready to scream. He gave me the number to the correct station, and I hung up before he could even say good-bye. I called the second station and again explained what was happening. They would send an officer over for a welfare check.

As I hung up with the police, the worrying came flooding out of me. Tears fell as my mind circled horrible thoughts that no parent needs to think. I was proud I was able to maintain my composure while talking to the police, but now I just needed the police to let me know she was OK. I kept calling Kyleigh's phone as I stood sobbing.

About five minutes later, my phone rang with a call from Kyleigh. I answered and Kyleigh said, "Police are here." And then quickly hung up. The tremendous relief I felt as I briefly heard her voice is indescribable. I didn't know what happened or where our dance had failed, but I knew she was alive and that was all I cared about at that moment.

Kyleigh later told me she had shut her phone off and accidentally forgot to turn it back on. I realized in that moment that if I hadn't called the police, she might have gone into a coma. Kyleigh said that the officers startled her from sleep and made her come outside to drink juice until her blood sugar went up. After noticing her weary, tired eyes and terrible bedhead, the officer said, "You poor girl!" Kyleigh looked at the phone and realized I had called twenty-eight times. Kyleigh replied to the officer, "No, my poor mother!" That was a bad night.

Kyleigh was tearful as she recounted the experience to me over the phone. I, too, was tearful knowing things could have ended differently. She was exhausted and appreciative of my persistence. I told her how much I loved her, and we made plans to speak in the morning to brainstorm about ways to prevent a recurrence in the future. We both said, "Good night. I love you," and hung up the phone. I wiped the tears from my cheeks, crawled into bed, and wished I could give each of my kids a hug.

As with any emotion, when we are presented with fear, we have the option to react, resist, or accept this emotion.

Anger and frustration can be a reaction to fear, leading to screaming, yelling, and other emotional outbursts. Reacting to fear can also lead to becoming obsessed with fearful thoughts which gives rise to anxiety. When the brain offers a thought, we work to find evidence to prove that thought. This is true even with fearful thoughts. We focus attention on fearful things to find more evidence to prove our thoughts. Unfortunately, this results in compounding the fear. This state of anxiety leaves us paralyzed and unable to take any action or make any progress because our brain is spinning with thoughts that are not useful.

Resisting fear can be pretending everything is fine. This is similar to someone attempting to keep a beach ball under water. They may be successful keeping it below the water's surface for a while, but eventually it comes flying up. We act like it's no big deal and we have the strength to handle anything. Resistance of fear eventually comes out in powerful, unexpected ways.

Accepting and processing fear as part of managing emotions can create an amazing life. We need to be able to experience fear without allowing it to control us. Managing emotions like fear is equivalent to treating a patient with an infection. Doctors must first understand the symptoms, then make the diagnosis to use the correct medicine to treat it. When we are first faced with fear, we need to look for symptoms and process the fear.

Learning Emotion Of Fear Through My Patient

I saw fear in others during my time as a doctor, too. I was a pediatrician in Hawaii when I first met a young family who had a baby boy in the Neonatal Intensive Care Unit. The mom's pregnancy was uneventful, but the baby was blue after birth instead of having vibrant pink skin. This physical exam finding can mean blood isn't getting the correct amount of oxygen. Thinking he may have a problem with his heart, his NICU team asked for an evaluation by a pediatric cardiologist. The evaluation indeed revealed a heart problem—transposition of the great arteries. This meant that the plumbing of his heart was connected backward, and his body was not able to get oxygenated blood. Babies will die without cardiac surgery. Until the child could safely get to the operating room, the infant needed a continuous infusion of prostaglandin. This medication keeps a cardiac connection open that usually closes after birth. This becomes a temporary life-saving measure to allow some mixing of blood so the child gets some oxygen.

The family knew all this information when I first met them. I came to see the infant and family because the heart surgery could not be done in Hawaii. He needed to be flown to Los Angeles, California, to have the surgery at LA Children's Hospital and a pediatrician could not leave his side during this transfer. I was asked to be that pediatrician. My role was to make sure he stayed sedated, continuously monitor his vital signs and ventilator, and not let the prostaglandin infusion stop.

I entered the NICU after the usual scrubbing and gowning was complete. I was shown to the infant's bed where the child was lying peacefully still with tubes, lines, and monitor leads draped over him like a pile of spaghetti as the only clue to just how sick he was. Looking past that pile of spaghetti, the infant was an angelic, beautiful boy with a round head full of dark baby hair and chubby cheeks, who appeared to be sleeping peacefully. His parents were next to him with the mother holding his hand to make sure the child knew he was loved. His mother and father were very young, I estimated in their early twenties. The father had dark hair just like his newborn son.

I introduced myself, as the mother wiped tears away from her cheeks. I asked if they understood the plan, and the father said they knew their son was going to be taken to California for heart surgery. I gave them some more details. We would take an ambulance to the local Air Force base in the morning. We would board a military plane that would fly from Hawaii to LAX airport. An ambulance would be waiting for us at LAX that would take us to LA Children's. I tried to make small talk, but it was clear they understood how serious and risky this transport would be. They also understood that the surgery and recovery would be challenging, but it was the only chance at life their son had. I did a quick physical exam on the infant and told the parents to try to get some rest before I'd see them in the morning.

That night, I packed a backpack with a change of clothes, toiletries, and a pediatric book I always carried as a resource for emergencies. Before walking out the door in the morning, I gave my children a kiss and grabbed my wallet. I double checked to make sure that I had my ID card and credit card. I loaded the car, but before I pulled out of the driveway, I decided to run back inside and grab $100 from the little bit of cash I kept for emergencies. I grabbed the money, put it in my wallet, and headed to the hospital.

The parents were already at the infant's bed when I got to the hospital. I wondered if they ever left because they looked tired, and the mom was once again wiping tears off her cheeks. The nurses already had the child loaded into an incubator that also functioned as his ventilator. I did my physical assessment, and as we waited to be told the ambulance was ready, I went over the medical details with the NICU team. We discussed the child's usual vital signs and ventilator settings. We checked the equipment I would be bringing to make sure we would have everything needed for emergencies. By the child's bed in the NICU were a nurse and a respiratory technician who would also be coming on the transport with me. We reviewed roles and knew we would be a team with one goal—a safe transport to LA Children's Hospital.

The ambulance was ready for us and as the leader of the team, I instructed everyone it was time to move. I put on my backpack and grabbed a medical supply bag while the respiratory technician grabbed the other supply bag. The nurse pushed the child's incubator as the parents followed behind to begin this journey across the Pacific Ocean.

We reached the ambulance, rolled the incubator onto the ambulance, and all of us loaded in, ready to move to the airport. Before we left the NICU, I informed the team I was going to perform a reassessment at each of our transition points during the transport. This was our first transition point, so I took out my stethoscope to begin a quick assessment before we drove off. Lungs were clear and equal, so the breathing tube had not moved. Vital signs were the same as the NICU, so the heart connection had not closed. I watched for a few seconds to make sure the prostaglandin infusion pump was still functioning smoothly. All was good, so I gave the thumbs up to the ambulance driver to head to the plane.

Our plane was waiting for us, and we carefully moved the incubator onto the plane and locked it into place. Once again, I performed my reassessment ritual to make sure nothing had become dislodged during the ambulance ride. Once again, there were no problems. The parents watched from their seats as I gave the thumbs up to the pilots. Soon we were in the air with the incubator in front of the seats that were occupied by the nurse, respiratory tech, and me. The parents sat a bit further away as instructed by the flight crew, but they could watch during the flight. The parents sat motionless. Having experienced it previously, I could easily recognize the overwhelmed, worried, zombie-like appearance on the parents' faces. If asked, I'm sure they would have said, "I'm fine."

Once we were in the air, problems arose. The aircraft was loud. My stethoscope proved useless during the flight because I couldn't hear the faint breath sounds to reassure me the child's breathing tube remained in the proper position. The pump and ventilator alarms also proved useless because their sound was drowned out by aircraft noise. This was concerning to me because if the pump or ventilator malfunctioned, I wouldn't know. I knew it would be bad if the child was not receiving his prostaglandin infusion or if the machine was not breathing for him while he was sedated. I quickly formulated a plan with the nurse and respiratory tech. We would take turns watching the pumping, watching the child's chest and ventilator, and resting. We would rotate tasks every thirty minutes. The five-hour flight from Hawaii to California was spent performing one of these three tasks. Thankfully, we never saw a problem during the flight, but I quickly pulled out my stethoscope after we landed and the loud noise stopped to ensure the child was doing well. All was good.

The ambulance was waiting for us. Once again, we loaded the incubator into the ambulance as the parents watched, but this time the ambulance driver approached me and said, "We can only take three people in the ambulance." I knew this meant the nurse, respiratory tech, and I would be riding in the ambulance, but the parents were left to find transportation to the hospital. I asked the ambulance driver how the parents were going to get to the hospital, and he said he didn't know, but a taxi was always available.

I walked over to the father and explained that he and his wife could not ride in the ambulance. I told him that the ambulance driver suggested taking a taxi to the hospital. I will never forget the look on the father's face. His face looked like he had seen a ghost. The fear was physically visible. I asked if he had money for a taxi. He couldn't speak and just shook his head no. I reached into my backpack, grabbed my wallet, and gave him the $100.

"Here, take this. Go get a taxi and I will meet you at the hospital. Your son is safe." The father's eyes filled with tears as he mumbled his thanks for taking care of his son.

I proceeded into the ambulance, performed another assessment, and gave the thumbs up to the ambulance driver to head to the hospital.

I knew the parents had been afraid and overwhelmed from the moment I met them, but in that moment with the father, the fear was so present that it became paralyzing.

After a safe arrival at the children's hospital, I handed off the baby to his new care team. They immediately began prepping the child for surgery and I reported that the parents would arrive shortly in a taxi from the airport. My team and I left and flew back to Hawaii not knowing the outcome of the child. I often thought about him and his parents hoping that they were enjoying the joys of parenthood instead of the stress of a long hospital stay. Several months later, I was taking care of patients in the outpatient pediatric clinic. I saw the baby's name on my schedule but was sure it couldn't be the same child. When I called his name from the waiting room, a big smile came across my face as I watched his parents rise from their chairs and push a stroller toward me. It was the beautiful baby I had transported. I hugged the parents and peeked into the stroller. There he was alive, smiling, chubby, and pink—not blue.

Lessons On Fear

Our life is constantly changing. No two days are exactly the same. Sometimes the sun is out and other days, it is rainy. Sometimes it snows and other days, it is windy. Just like the weather, humans are constantly growing and evolving. We have a choice, though, in how this happens.

Parents can feel overwhelmed with the unpredictability of a child's actions or behavior. A simple trip to the grocery store can quickly turn into a nightmare when a child throws a fit because they want a candy bar. This unpredictability becomes more complex when a child has a medical challenge such as autism or Down syndrome. A parent is left feeling fearful, helpless, and defeated with thoughts that they cannot change their life.

Chronic illness can be scary for both children and parents but being a parent of a child with medical needs does not mean that you can't lead a full, complete life. It's natural for parents of chronically ill children to feel fear. Without tons of experience, parents have difficulty knowing what to do when a child is sick, but fear can make everything more difficult. Fear of the unknown, fear of what might happen next, and fear for their child's well-being can be all-consuming. Managing fear is an important part of taking care of a child with medical challenges. Maintaining inner calmness and a hopeful demeanor during these tough times is essential to successfully navigate to the other side of the obstacle.

Our journey in life is like riding around in a car. When we believe that life can't change because fear is in control, we are in the driver's seat but our hands are not on the steering wheel. We are a passenger in a car that is driving itself. The car is swerving and turning without any input from us. The ride is frightening as we watch, hoping we don't wreck. The belief that life can change is what allows us to grab the wheel of the car and lead it down a path. There is still some fear and unpredictability to the journey, such as a police officer hiding around a turn, but we manage our fear because we are in control and going the speed limit.

Changing our life is in our control. Grabbing the wheel of the car involves learning to set goals, create habits, and be aware of thoughts and feelings. This takes practice and change can be slow, but patience can result in significant progress if we commit to moving in the right direction. The grocery store trip no longer needs to be a nightmare but can turn into time to enjoy your child who is getting to explore something new.

Learning these tools changed my life. I am proof that life can change. My life is very different compared to a few years ago. I have big goals that I am committed to achieve. I feel fulfilled and enjoy the relationships that are important to me. I am organized in how I use my time and I am very aware of my thoughts. Sadly, the conditions of my life haven't changed, and my child's health challenges will be constantly present. I still hope for a magic cure to Kyleigh's diabetes. I still worry about my child, but my life changed when I stopped letting fear drive the car, and instead I took hold of the steering wheel.

Here are four ways to begin managing the emotion of fear.

1. **BE CURIOUS AND AWARE OF YOUR THOUGHTS.** Avoid judging yourself with thoughts such as, *You shouldn't be afraid.* Ask yourself

what is scaring you and acknowledge the thoughts causing the fear. When I wasn't able to quickly reach Kyleigh when her blood sugar was low, I feared she was in a coma or dead. As I was trying to reach the police, my head spun with thoughts like, *This is silly. She is fine. You are over-reacting.* These thoughts, though, made the fear worse, believing Kyleigh would be upset because I overreacted. Controlling my thoughts to be intentional about my actions in the moment was important.

2. **SEPARATE STORY FROM FACT.** It isn't unusual to be afraid of something that hasn't occurred. The overwhelming fear I experienced when awaiting Kyleigh's c-myc test result was from thinking about the risks of a bone marrow transplant. The bone marrow transplant wasn't occurring. It wasn't even part of the treatment plan, but it was driving my fear. This awareness can help change our thoughts.

3. **FEEL THE EMOTION.** Acknowledge that you are afraid, breathe, and allow yourself to experience fear. Fear creates physical symptoms in your body, but it doesn't mean we are in danger. When I transported the sick baby to LA Children's, the father of my sick patient was not in danger. He didn't have money for a taxi, and he didn't know what was going to happen to his son, but the father was physically safe. Fear, though, was obviously present, evident by his physical appearance. It becomes important

during times like this, to acknowledge the fear and experience it without becoming consumed with it.

4. **FOCUS ON POSITIVE OUTCOMES.** Practice calmness and peace by practicing gratitude. This helps shift the mind into a positive light, extinguishing the negative light of fear. Focusing my mind on Kyleigh's successful surgery and smooth recovery would have allowed me to be grateful for what had already occurred rather than afraid for what had not yet occurred.

It is impossible to eliminate all fear from our lives because we are human, but we can manage it and keep moving forward. Talking to other parents who have gone through similar experiences can help cultivate peace and calmness. Other individuals who have walked a similar road can be a valuable source of support. Professional help can also provide guidance and support when working to move forward. Taking care of yourself mentally and emotionally will give you the strength and courage to face adversity. Even as a doctor, it was only when I learned to face fear that I was able to take care of myself properly.

We are never stuck in life. The conditions of life may never change, but how we think, feel, and respond to them are in our control. The results created when we take charge and drive the car can be amazing. Our brain can work against us, but it can become an incredible gift if we learn to control it. This is how life changes. This is how we grab the steering wheel.

Chapter 6

GUILT

Parents of chronically ill children can feel overwhelming guilt wash over them, making it difficult to think or move forward. It is important to manage and move past those feelings to continue living a full life for yourself and your child.

We can experience a full spectrum of feelings with some being useful and others being uncomfortable and useless. Each feeling is anchored in a thought the brain has offered. Guilt, for example, can be experienced when the brain is telling us we are responsible for our child's chronic illness or that we "should have" done something different in the past.

Learning Emotion Of Guilt Through Kyleigh

As a baby, Kyleigh recovered from her lengthy surgery in the Pediatric ICU. Each day, she became stronger with less pain. Tubes and lines were slowly removed, and Kyleigh was soon transferred to the inpatient pediatric ward. Kyleigh still needed to go back to the operating room for placement of a central line to receive her first dose of chemotherapy. I remained worried yet optimistic as we continued to take steps closer to the goal of discharge.

While on the pediatric ward, I took Kyleigh on walks down the hall to keep her entertained, especially when she got fussy. Selfishly, it was also my time to get out of the tiny hospital room and interact with nurses and other parents. Staring at the same four walls made my mind spin, and I was missed the personal connection I made with my patients and families in the clinic.

One day on my walk, I saw a GI doctor that I knew with his wife and asked if everything was OK. He explained his young son was being admitted for frequent vomiting. The physicians taking care of the boy wanted to obtain a CT scan of his head. I knew immediately that the physicians must be concerned about a brain tumor. Increased pressure in someone's head can cause vomiting so this was something that needed to be ruled out. "Keep me posted!" I said as I continued my walk.

As I walked away from the couple, I said a prayer hoping that their luck would be better than mine. I prayed that the vomiting was a common case of gastroenteritis and the young boy only needed some IV fluids to resolve dehydration. The next day on my hallway walk, I knew my prayers weren't answered in the way I had hoped. I saw the wife of the physician at the nurse's station. She was asking for some ice chips. I came next to her with Kyleigh in my arms and said, "Good morning," and as she turned toward me to respond, I could see her bright red eyes. Those eyes told me everything.

"It's a brain tumor," she said, and went on to say that he would require surgery. The CT scan results came back the day prior and the team of physicians were making a treatment plan for the boy. The woman explained that no one was sure about the next steps after surgery because they needed to know the specific type of tumor, but chemotherapy and maybe radiation could be part of the treatment plan. My heart broke for her as she stood waiting for the ice chips.

I didn't see the family during the remainder of Kyleigh's inpatient stay because the boy was moved to the Pediatric ICU for closer monitoring before and after his surgery. I saw them again, though, a few weeks later in the Pediatric Oncology clinic waiting with me for the boy's follow-up appointment. The boy's head was shaved, and the healing incision marks were still visible. The mom, like me, was in zombie mode. She explained what type of tumor it was, and the boy was on a chemotherapy protocol. I joked that this meant we could see lots of each other. The mother chuckled and said, "Sadly for both of us…yes."

We saw each other frequently in the waiting room and on the inpatient ward. It felt like we were living between those two places. The young boy, though, had lots of problems with his treatment. I began dreading bumping into them because with each encounter, the boy appeared more and more sickly. I became embarrassed. I was sure the mother was thinking that the differences in chemotherapy side effects between Kyleigh and the boy weren't fair. Chemo wasn't fun and Kyleigh had her challenges, but I felt her challenges were nothing compared to the challenges my GI friend's boy faced.

I realized I enjoyed seeing them at the start of the journey because we were supportive of each other's situation. We understood the initiation into the club of parents of sick children. We were able to vent and share our experiences, but what I did not anticipate as part of this bond was the guilt. I dreaded seeing the family because I felt guilty for how different our paths were. Kyleigh's prognosis was good, the boy's prognosis was not. Kyleigh was tolerating her chemo without major issues, but the boy was not. The bond that initially united us was now the thing caused me guilt.

The boy lost his life to his tumor. The news of his passing hit me hard. I felt like the mother and I began a marathon together, but her race ended before she got to the finish line. Why was I allowed to continue the race with Kyleigh? It all just seemed so unfair. The guilt I experienced previously grew after his passing, as I continued on the marathon race.

Guilt appeared again when Kyleigh was fifteen. Kyleigh and I went to all her endocrinology appointments together. They always were the same—take vital signs and check Kyleigh's weight, check a hemoglobin A1C, look at past blood sugar numbers, calculate how much insulin was being used, and adjust her pump. Kyleigh hated the appointments and dreaded them as they approached. This time was not any different.

We went to the appointment and Kyleigh was anxious about her hemoglobin A1C number. She decided that we would make it fun and if the number was below 7.0, then I would take her to dinner after the appointment. Deal! Kyleigh's vital signs looked good, and her weight was appropriate. Now the hemoglobin A1C check—6.9. It was fun to watch Kyleigh glow with confidence and the anxiety melt away. She'd won the bet, but I knew it was her health she was really happy about.

During the appointment the physician looked closely at Kyleigh's numbers. "Kyleigh, what happened on Monday at lunch? It looks like your blood sugar was high. Did you count carbs correctly?" Kyleigh shrugged. The physician continued her analysis of Kyleigh's blood sugar history and said, "Kyleigh, did something happen late afternoon last Wednesday? It looks like you went low. I wonder if that was from too much insulin at lunch or a change in activity that day. Any ideas?" Kyleigh shrugged again. With each question, I slowly watched Kyleigh's glow fade. Her face became still and stoic. I thought it was odd because I didn't think the questions were too difficult. Having been a pediatrician, I asked similar questions to my diabetic patients.

The endocrinologist's final question made it clear to me that Kyleigh wasn't being a good diabetic. The physician asked if the low blood sugar on Tuesday morning was because she forgot to have breakfast. With a blank stare, Kyleigh shrugged her shoulders again and didn't mumble a word. *This is crazy!* I thought to myself, *How can my own daughter not know if there was anything special that caused her high and low blood sugars?*

We finished the visit, loaded into the car, and ventured to Kyleigh's choice of restaurants, a Brazilian steakhouse. On the way to the restaurant, I felt like I needed to chat with Kyleigh before we celebrated her diabetic accomplishment. I began the conversation with praise and made sure that Kyleigh knew I was proud of how she was taking care of herself. I went on to explain, though, that I knew she could do better. I told her about how challenging it is as a physician to make insulin adjustments if the patient doesn't offer some clinical history to help guide the process.

"If you check your sugar and it's high, I want you to think back to your last meal and make sure you are confident in the number of carbs you estimated," I said.

Kyleigh sat quietly as I continued to drive and talk.

"If you check your sugar and it is low, don't just make sure you have enough carbs to bring it back up, but take an extra step and jot down if there was something different that went on to make your sugar go low."

Kyleigh continued to be silent.

"I'm not say you are doing a bad job. You are doing great with managing your sugars! I just want you to take the next step to help tighten your control."

Kyleigh's silence now turned into sniffling. I quickly glanced over at her and saw tears coming down her cheeks. "What's the matter?" I asked with concern. I couldn't figure out anything I said that was insensitive. Quite the contrary, I was offering her advice to help make progress and make the endocrinology visits more productive.

Kyleigh finally spoke through tears, "Mom, I think about diabetes *all the time*! I can't even have a snack without thinking about it. I can't think about it anymore than I do now. I want to think about teen stuff, and I can't if I spend all my time thinking about diabetes."

She was correct. She didn't have the usual life of a child. She spent a lot of brain power on managing insulin so she could eat without killing herself. Kyleigh's ability to think like a child was stolen on the day that she was diagnosed with diabetes. I couldn't believe how small I felt in that moment. I felt guilty for not recognizing that kids shouldn't be expected to be "good diabetics." I felt guilty for expecting my patients *and* my daughter to have a physician's brain and diagnose blood sugar swings in moments like lunch in the school cafeteria or dance class in the studio. This was an absurd expectation, and I felt guilty for ever possessing it.

I had reached the restaurant and pulled into a parking space quickly reaching over to hug Kyleigh. I wiped the tears from her cheeks and apologized to her. We were able to share laughs over dinner despite the cloud of guilt that hung over my head.

Learning Emotion Of Guilt Through My Patient

I loved working with LaRon. He was an outstanding pediatric clinic nurse that one day asked me to care for his son. I was honored. Brian was in fifth grade at the time, and I was excited to meet him. He was having trouble in school and LaRon and his wife wanted me to help.

When Brian came into clinic, he was polite and initially shy as I introduced myself. He sat on the exam table as his mother spoke. She explained that Brian was performing poorly in school because he was not turning in his work and was getting in trouble during class for not paying attention. I continued to ask her questions about Brian including things like sleep, behavior at home, and other symptoms. Brian was having trouble completing chores at home and was so fidgety during church services that it was causing the family to dislike attending. I had a laundry list of ideas that might be the underlying cause including thyroid problems, depression, learning disability, and attention-deficit disorder. As Brian's mom and I spoke, I could hear the rustling and tearing of the exam table paper in the background. Brian's mom kept interrupting herself, telling him to sit still. The mom continued to talk and out of the corner of my eye, I saw little exam paper balls whiz by me. The mom got up as she continued to talk and took a seat next to Brian holding his hands so he would stop the fidgeting. She spoke fast and had a lot to say. I observed that she covered an array of topics about Brian without me even asking a question. She would tell a story about Brian during this academic year and without transitioning, she would switch to a story of his earlier childhood only to switch back to present time. She was very kind and we had moments of laughter in the conversation.

After I heard all the concerns and gathered the full history, I did an exam on Brian. The exam was normal with excellent growth and healthy vital signs. Based on the mother's story, I concluded that it was probably ADD, but I needed more data. I discussed my concerns with Brian and his mother and gave them questionnaires that needed to be completed by each parent and his teacher. I arranged a follow-up visit to discuss the completed questionnaires.

The result of the questionnaires confirmed my suspicion for ADD. The questionnaires showed he was not anxious, depressed, or displaying any other conduct concerns. They simply confirmed his impulsivity and inattentiveness. I explained the results of the data to Brian with his mother listening. I wanted to discuss treatment options and asked Brian if he could have a seat in the waiting room so his mom and I could focus on a plan. He agreed and left the room, having a seat just outside the door.

I began explaining treatment options of ADD including behavioral therapies, 504 school plans, and medications. I was gentle in my approach, as I always was, to make sure Brian's mom did not feel like I was condemning her child with the diagnosis. I wanted her to understand that the diagnosis wasn't "labeling" him, but rather giving a name to something that made Brian unique and to better equip everyone with the tools that would allow Brian to thrive. I continued explaining how this seemed like a challenge now, but it was really a gift. He could use his active mind to be creative, find unique solutions to problems, or experience many different things in life.

I noticed tears now running down her cheeks and for the first time, she was quiet. I paused and asked if everything was OK. She responded with a myriad of thoughts:

She should have realized this sooner so he wouldn't have experienced the problems in school.

She should have not been so strict with him at home when he didn't finish his chores because he got distracted.

She should have encouraged him to do more sports to consume his energy.

The tears really flowed when she told me that this was her fault.

She was overwhelmed with guilt.

I listened to all her thoughts and recognized them as the ones I experienced previously with Kyleigh. I offered her tissues. I quickly realized that Brian needed my help, but so did Brian's mom. In order to help Brian improve his school performance, I needed to help Brian's mom process guilt and focus on being an exceptional parent. In residency, I learned about "vulnerable child syndrome" when a parent overcompensates for the guilt they feel—resulting in poor parenting. This was something I was very conscious to avoid when Kyleigh was sick. As I listened to Brian's mom, I knew the guilt could cause her to avoid setting expectations, give him a tremendous amount of free reign, and not enjoy parenting her son. As we spoke, I was once again reminded of the fast, tangential speech pattern of Brian's mom. I listened and said, "Yes, Brian has ADD, but you probably do, too." She paused and laughed with the realization that she indeed had difficulty focusing.

I reminded her of her very successful life and that she has given him an incredible gift, not a curse.

This empowering thought was the basis of an incredible partnership. I watched as Brian was able to grow and thrive in school, and Brian's mom was able to grow and thrive at being his mom. Her guilt transformed into support and confidence. She was a fantastic parent.

Lessons On Guilt

Oftentimes when parents receive the news of a chronic diagnosis, an endless mental cycle occurs from feeling guilty and continuing to question, "Why is this happening to us?" The result is the creation of more guilt.

Life isn't always filled with roses and unicorns. We know this all too well as parents of a chronically ill child. When we are in the middle of a challenging part of life, it becomes easy to have thoughts such as, *Only bad things happen to me!* or *The universe never gives me a break!* We start focusing on only the negative and we lose perspective, forcing us further into despair.

Imagine a painting that had one dot in the middle of a giant canvas and beautiful flowers around the edge. If you stand up close to the painting and only stare at the dot, you lose perspective. Standing back and looking at the entire painting allows you to appreciate a beautiful work of art that is created by a combination of a boring dot and incredible flowers.

Life is equivalent to this beautiful artwork. It is full of good things and bad things leading us to feel good emotions along with uncomfortable emotions. This is the full human experience. We don't appreciate this, though, if we don't stand back and see both the good and the bad.

The creation of useful emotions is accomplished by managing our mind. Managing our mind allows us to control our emotions rather than allow emotions to control our future. As parents, we first need to accept that the past cannot be changed as an initial step to overcome guilt. No matter how much we may want, we have no control over the events we are given in our lives, and we cannot go back in time to change the hand we were dealt. I had no control over Kyleigh's diagnosis of neuroblastoma or diabetes. I couldn't change how the universe wrote Kyleigh's story. It is empowering, though, to realize that we do have control over the mind and can change the thoughts we have about past events. Living in the past keeps us stuck, but we can control the present and future.

Guilt is a normal emotion, but with any emotion, processing the feeling is important to become forward focused. Processing guilt is bringing awareness to the emotion and allowing it rather than trying to get rid of it. Uncomfortable emotions give us a full-life experience. No one enjoys experiencing discomfort, but it is through this discomfort that we can find power. As we bring awareness to the emotion of guilt, we can understand how our mind is creating this feeling. Through awareness, we can decide how to think, feel, and act about our child's chronic illness. This gives us power.

Allowing the emotion of guilt and focusing your mind on productive questions will lead to redirecting attention to useful thoughts that will break the cycle. Your mind can sometimes function as a bully forcing you to stay stagnant.

The answers to the B-U-L-L-Y questions will allow you to stand up and take control of your mind.

(B) What can I <u>Build</u> from this experience?

(U) How can I <u>Use</u> this to make me a more resilient person?

(L) What are the <u>Lessons</u> I can learn by living this experience?

(L) How do I want my <u>Life</u> to change?

(Y) Why are <u>You</u> the perfect person for this to happen to?

Brian's mom learned that she could build Brian's confidence since she was successfully navigating life with the same diagnosis. She could use her own past experiences to help her be confident in parenting Brian at home and advocating for him at school. Brian's mom learned she needed to work on her own patience when parenting Brian. She realized how self-awareness and calmness were needed to change her life. She was the perfect mother for Brian.

Pretend for a moment that life is only full of good. It would be boring. We would never be able to cherish or appreciate the good because we would only know one side. Instead, life is half good and half bad allowing us to experience an entire spectrum of emotions. The contrast between good and bad gives us the opportunity to intensely feel the good and fully appreciate it.

No parent wants to watch their child struggle with neuroblastoma or diabetes or ADHD, but I am comforted by my belief about life being both good and bad. Fully experiencing the negative emotions now, such as guilt, allows a full experience of the good emotions later. I was able to process my sadness around my child's struggles, and I was able to maintain perspective that this is just a boring dot on a beautiful piece of art.

I am glad that life is not all bad, but I am just as grateful that life isn't all good. Life is a roller coaster with ups and downs, but this is exactly what makes it exciting and worth the ride. Cherish the good, but don't forget to appreciate the bad. It is all part of the journey. Knowing how to process and move through discomfort is the magical key to living an extraordinary life despite challenging situations with our children.

Chapter 7

RESENTMENT

> *"What we don't recognize is that holding onto resentment is like holding onto your breath. You'll soon start to suffocate."* – *Deepak Chopra*

Webster's dictionary defines *resentment* as "a feeling of indignant displeasure or persistent ill will at something regarded as a wrong, insult, or injury." Resentment can be described as feeling disappointed, angry, outraged, and disgusted. The word is synonymous with anger, spite, and holding a grudge and originates from the French word "ressentir.". The prefix *re-* means "again", and *sentir* "to feel." The feeling of resentment is a result of a previous emotional injury which is now being "felt again." It is provoked by thoughts our brains offer about circumstances that involve a sense of injustice or wrongdoing.

Learning The Emotion Of Resentment Through Kyleigh

After Kyleigh completed her final chemotherapy treatment as a baby, it was time to return to work. I had been on a leave of absence from my residency training for months to care for Kyleigh. I had mixed feelings about returning. I was excited to return to learning my passion of medicine, but I felt sad and guilty for leaving my young child when I had just learned the incredible lesson of not taking for granted the precious moments I was given with her. The decision, though, was very simple. So simple, in fact, that it didn't feel like I even had a choice. I was in the military so if I didn't return to work, I would be considered AWOL (absent without leave) which would mean significant consequences. I resumed my residency training that Monday.

Monday morning I got dressed in my uniform, packed up my things, kissed my babies goodbye, and headed to the hospital. I was filled with many emotions as I drove to work that day. Feelings of excitement came from thoughts of seeing my colleagues. Feelings of nervousness came from wondering if I was going to be behind my peers due to my prolonged absence.

I was welcomed back at morning report and then I began an outpatient clinic rotation. During this rotation, residents were expected to see and evaluate the patient and then discuss the case with the attending physician. My program director thought this rotation would ease me back into medicine by being able to evaluate lots of patients without the stress that inpatient medicine brings. I was grateful.

My first patient was a three-year-old boy with an ear infection. *I've got this!* I told myself. It went flawlessly. The next patient was school-aged child for an asthma check. *I can do this*, the voice inside my head told me. Another success. Then the third patient was a child who was the same age as Kyleigh. The mother brought the child in for the chief complaint of a rash. The mother explained that the rash developed the previous night and looked like pink spots all over the young boy's body. *Easy*, the voice said, but for some reason I started thinking of Kyleigh and her neuroblastoma. It made me uneasy, so I pushed it from my mind.

"Did they itch?" I asked. The mother explained that they didn't seem to bother the boy.

"Can I see the rash?" I asked. The mother went on to tell me the rash was gone when the child woke up that morning.

"Could it have been an allergy?" the mother asked. She then continued with a laundry list of possibilities she thought might have caused this fleeting rash.

As she was rattling off her list of possible causes, I started feeling tremendous resentment toward this mother and child. Her list included food allergy, irritation from a detergent, she had tried a new soap, he played outside in the grass the day prior, and so on. Not once did neuroblastoma appear on her list. It shouldn't have, but the fact that it was absent made me want to scream.

Did this lady realize what I had just been through? Did she realize my child could have died and still may because she was fighting cancer? Did the mom in my office understand the challenges of caring for a sick child at home? Her child's fleeting rash did not come close to the horror I had experienced over the previous months. I would have given anything to trade neuroblastoma for a rash that disappeared overnight.

I took care of the child by prescribing some moisturizer and oatmeal baths and quickly sent them on their way. The visit was brief and not filled with my usual cordialities. The mom had never had a visit with me before so I'm sure she didn't notice a difference, but I did. I was curt, to the point, and heartless. I was angry.

Kyleigh hated diabetes and so did I. I realized it the moment I diagnosed her in that tiny school bathroom. That diagnosis changed everything about every day for the remainder of her life. She couldn't put food in her mouth without thinking of diabetes. Diabetes woke her from her sleep. Diabetes needed to be on her mind whenever she was leaving the house so she was prepared for blood sugar swings.

The part of diabetes, though, that we both hated was how blood sugar swings made Kyleigh feel. High blood sugars caused her to be on edge. She used pressured speech and the world needed to keep up with the fast pace of her mind. She made mistakes easily if doing schoolwork because the uncontrolled speed resulted in carelessness. Low blood sugars caused her to be cranky and ravenous. She easily became emotional and very sluggish.

The blood sugar swings complicated parenting a sixteen-year-old going through puberty. It was challenging to determine if Kyleigh was on edge from high blood sugar or PMS. Was she having a sudden onset of crying because of a bad day at school or was her blood sugar low? Was the laziness I was observing was adolescent ambivalence or a blood sugar swing?

Another part we both disliked were outbursts. She snapped and lashed out at me over small things like asking about homework or commenting on makeup. Sometimes it was in a subtle way with sassiness, and other times it was more overt with yelling and slamming doors. Never, though, did these outbursts happen with others. I observed Kyleigh at school or at a store and she got frustrated, but never had one of her outbursts. The moodiness only happened with me.

The outbursts always ended in apologizing and acknowledging our dislike of diabetes. One day we had a candid discussion of the moodiness and seemingly uncontrollable behavioral outbursts. I told Kyleigh it seemed like she only got upset with me. My heart broke as she agreed. Though it hurt to hear, Kyleigh resented being a diabetic. She went on to help me understand that controlling her actions was incredibly challenging during times of blood sugar swings. It was exhausting and made the high or low much more difficult to manage while simultaneously trying to manage overt behavior. She went on to explain that she knew my love for her was unconditional. I would love her even if a door slammed or if she was snappy.

As she explained her behavior to me, I understood. I was happy she loved me enough to feel comfortable letting her guard down, but I was angry and resentful of the disease that made parenting even more challenging. Teenage years were already a struggle, especially with the overlay of the hormonal changes of puberty. I hated the blood sugar struggle that forced me to take on the additional role of an emotional punching bag.

Kyleigh and I both resented the universe for placing diabetes in our lives. I knew we both needed to process this emotion before it consumed us. Thankfully, we both have successfully processed our resentment, but it does pop up occasionally, especially when Kyleigh's having a difficult day managing her blood sugar.

Learning The Emotion Of Resentment Through My Patient

As a physician, I spent my career caring for patients and educating young physicians. My role was to mold physicians-in-training into independent, confident doctors. I was always passionate about teaching and knew the importance of educating physicians about mistakes.

Mistakes are an inevitable part of medicine. Doctors are humans and humans are not perfect. Our medical community puts systems in place to help prevent errors, but they still occur. My educator mind wanted to make sure that young physicians knew they would not always be perfect and that mistakes were part of the job. I knew the danger of continuing to instill perfectionism. The idea that physicians are always perfect has led to a high rate of burnout since it became a mortal injury to make a mistake. It was my role as a leader and mentor to normalize imperfections and discuss them in a safe, non-punitive way, allowing the opportunity to learn from each other's mistakes.

Part of the internship curriculum I developed was a project called "My Mistake." Each intern needed to pick one mistake in which they were involved and give a 10–15 minute presentation to the internship group on the error. In addition to discussing the mistake, each intern was given feedback by their peers on their oral presentation skills. This assignment helped to develop interns into providers who could comfortably discuss medical errors in an open, professional way. It was brilliant!

One afternoon, our internship group was gathered to hear from some of the physicians about their mistakes. Most were fairly commonplace. The first intern presented and told the story of how he wrote an order on the wrong patient. The second intern presented and discussed how she read an x-ray incorrectly. But the third intern's presentation led me to experience unexpected resentment.

She began her presentation something that occurred while she was on call. She had admitted a patient with type 1 diabetes who managed her blood sugar with an insulin pump. The nurses asked the intern for orders to help them know what to do with the insulin pump. The intern explained she didn't know anything about a pump. The intern didn't want to bother the endocrinology team, so she decided to discontinue the pump until the morning when the endocrinology team could give better instructions. The following morning, the patient's blood sugar was very high, and the endocrinology team was very upset with the intern.

At the end of the presentation, the intern began discussing lessons learned. The first lesson she presented to the group was, "I hate insulin pumps." The audience of interns laughed, but a wave of resentment washed over me. What did she say? Did I hear her correctly? Did she know who she was presenting to? Was she saying that she disliked the tool that saved Kyleigh from multiple sticks along with maintaining better blood sugar control? A million thoughts raced through my mind as I continued to process her lesson.

When she finished her presentation, I sternly asked, "So you hate insulin pumps?" The intern did not realize that my mood had changed and casually responded, "Yeah, they're just so complicated." A couple of interns in the audience chuckled while others noticed that I didn't crack a smile. Resentment had taken control of my actions. We spent the remainder of the session discussing insulin pumps and how ignorance in medicine shouldn't drive our actions. The discussion was not my usual engaging lecture, but more like a parental lecture when a child has done something wrong. I was filled with resentment and anger. Everyone in the room knew it. That week's session ended abruptly without the usual post-session chit-chat. I had let resentment deprive us of an opportunity to network and build community.

Lessons On Resentment

When we think that something has happened to us outside of our control, the initial emotion created is anger. If that anger continues without awareness and processing, resentment occurs. Resentment causes us to become preoccupied with thoughts of being wronged, further escalating our emotion. It is always destructive and leads to unintended results such as disrupted relationships between family members, colleagues, or friends. Kyleigh's resentment with diabetes was disrupting our mother-daughter relationship. It is an emotion that will not drive positive actions, but instead it can be emotionally and physically destructive and difficult to overcome if it is allowed to fester. It can rob us of our joy.

Practicing self-awareness is an important tool to overcome resentment. We need to be aware our mind is creating a story that is causing us to feel wronged. It can be helpful to have a non-judgmental perspective of our own mind and gain an understanding of the thoughts driving the resentment by asking questions such as, "What is causing the disappointment?"

When I returned to work after Kyleigh's chemotherapy course was complete, my anger stemmed from thoughts that my child's medical problems were not fair. It was an injustice that I was forced to watch my daughter suffer and hope she survived. Comparing my problems to those of others led me to minimize the problems of others and resent the circumstances I was given. I compared my child's medical problems to a child seeking treatment for a mild rash and became flooded with resentment. I knew I needed to reign in my feelings of resentment before it extinguished the fire I had to be a great pediatrician.

Here are three steps to begin overcoming resentment.

1. **ACKNOWLEDGE YOUR RESENTMENT.** Recognizing you're feeling resentment is the first step in managing it. You can only start to address it if you identify the emotion you are feeling. I was terse in my visit with the mother who brought her child to see me for a rash. I was angry and resentful.

2. **UNDERSTAND YOUR RESENTMENT.** What event or situation led to the resentment? Why do you feel like this person or situation deserves your resentment? An understanding of the root cause of the resentment can lead you to take steps to resolve it. I felt resentment because I thought it was unfair to struggle with pediatric cancer rather than a simple rash.

3. **FORGIVE THE PERSON OR SITUATION.** This doesn't mean what they did was OK. This doesn't mean you believe the situation is easy to handle. Forgiveness is necessary, though, to release the resentment and move on. I knew I needed to actively choose to let go of my resentment and forgive the universe for giving my daughter a medical challenge.

4. **ACT.** If the resentment is due to a specific event or situation, there may be some steps you need to take to

resolve the issue. This could involve talking to the person involved or setting boundaries. The action I took was actively changing my thoughts. I understood I was given a daughter with medical issues because I could handle it. The experience gave me a deeper understanding of my patients. The mother bringing her child in for a simple rash wasn't wasting my time. She came to the clinic to get medical help because she was worried. I knew I had the medical knowledge to resolve her concern. The new belief melted away the resentment.

Tony Robbins once said, "It is in your moments of decision that your destiny is shaped." I feel fortunate I had the gift of self-awareness during this early point in my career and could see that a decision could propel my life forward. I intentionally chose to stay in medicine because I realized Kyleigh's medical problems were a gift that could make me a better doctor. I worked to understand my patients rather than resent them. Parents were coming to see me because they were worried about their child just like I worried about my daughter. This understanding allowed me to regenerate my passion and focus. I have had a remarkable medical career because I was able to intentionally decide to get unstuck.

Similarly, I was able to use these steps to get unstuck during my time as a physician educator. I was aware of my feelings of anger and resentment toward my intern who nonchalantly dismissed insulin pumps. I understood that I felt resentment because this was an important tool in my child's life, but I quickly forgave the intern for her ignorance. I realized that the intern's public dislike of an important medical tool was actually a gift. It allowed me the opportunity to educate a room full of young physicians. This wouldn't have happened if her ignorance remained silent. I became even more passionate about education and once again, intentionally decided to move forward.

Actions and Results

Chapter 8

MAINTAINING PERSPECTIVE

> *"To change ourselves effectively, we first had to change our perceptions."* – Stephen R. Covey

When we ride on a roller coaster, we experience fear and anxiety as the train climbs the steep hill, but as the train comes racing down the track and makes our belly drop, we soon find ourselves laughing and smiling over the extreme exuberance. The roller coaster ride eventually ends and instantly we want to get back in line and ride again knowing that the pleasure of the fun moment was worth the price of the intense fear. The ups and downs we experience on this amusement ride is similar to the ups and downs we experience in life. Everyone's life is full of joy along with disappointment. Kyleigh's medical problems had a significant impact on me, and there have been other stressful times. But I lead a beautiful life. I have grown from each experience and appreciate the beauty of the wonderful times in life, but I am also able to experience the difficult times without hiding from my emotions.

Perspective is the ability to understand another individual and consider their thoughts and emotions or gain a different point of view. Perspective brings in the mindfulness of compassion and empathy to our relationships. Understanding our children will also experience thoughts and feelings that fuel their actions will allow us to intervene in a way that helps our children in the moment and in the future. The ability to have perspective relies on the understanding of ourselves and ability to manage our own mind.

Learning About The Action And Result Of Maintaining Perspective Through Kyleigh

The months of chemotherapy when Kyleigh was a baby were challenging. There were follow-up appointments, more trips back to the operating room for central lines and replacement central lines, and admissions to the pediatric ward to administer the chemo. I watched as my happy, portly child became a skinny, cranky baby. It was torture.

At her appointments, she needed blood work. If her line was functional, the nurse obtained her blood work using the central line. Sometimes, though, the line wasn't cooperating, so the blood work required a usual blood draw from a vein in her arm. I sat in the little clinic waiting room and wondered which it was going to be on that day—the painless draw through the line or the painful poke in a vein. When it was time, the nurse came and took Kyleigh to the exam room next door and I listened. If all was quiet, the line was working. If there was screaming, she was getting poked. Her screams were her words, and I wish I could have covered my ears so I didn't have to hear them.

Kyleigh's screams became more frequent and started even prior to getting stuck. A month or two into the chemotherapy regimen, Kyleigh had a fever. She recently received chemotherapy and I knew this meant she was getting admitted for a neutropenic fever. Neutropenia is when a patient's infection fight cells (white blood cells) are low. It occurs as a consequence of chemotherapy and makes a patient more prone to infections. A fever can be a sign of infection which is very dangerous during neutropenic times because the immune system doesn't have the cells it needs to fight. It always requires admission in young infants. We were admitted to the pediatrics ward and a few days later, Kyleigh's dad came to sit with her while I went home to eat, shower, and recharge for a few hours. I left the hospital room when he arrived, and I passed the baton. I walked down the hall and ear-piercing screams came from Kyleigh's room.

I wanted to run back but knew that she was not screaming because she was in pain. She was safe, but this was her way of expressing emotion. She had learned that every time she was away from me, someone would poke or prod her. Her screams were expressions of fear because she thought it was going to happen again when I left her hospital room. My heart ached as her screams echoed down the hall.

Reflecting on the time of Kyleigh's neuroblastoma, I am very grateful for her inability to speak. Her screams were enough to know her emotions were those of fear and discomfort. Hearing her words would have made it worse for me as a parent. It was moments like this that gave me the understanding that even infants have actions resulting from emotion. Being aware of Kyleigh's perspective allowed me to reconcile my own emotions. Even though her screams made my heart break, I felt comfortable continuing to walk down the hall. I understood I was allowing my child to build resilience even as an infant by not racing back to save her. I was also allowing time to recharge myself so I could return and do an even better job of caring for Kyleigh.

When Kyleigh was an infant with neuroblastoma, I guessed her thoughts based on how she acted, since she was not verbal. By the time Kyleigh was diagnosed with diabetes, she was thoughtful, intelligent, and well-spoken. At twelve years old, her thoughts were no secret. There were times I wished I didn't know what she was thinking, but in retrospect, understanding her perspective allowed me to support her better as a parent.

Two weeks after her diabetes diagnosis, I picked Kyleigh up around dinner time from ballet because she had a late practice. She had a pretty good day and her blood sugars were cooperative that day, but she was starving when she jumped into the car. We had a forty-five-minute drive home and she begged me to stop for food somewhere because the journey home was too long. The only place close was a fast-food restaurant so we decided to visit the drive thru.

I pulled the car around to the large menu that was displayed at the microphone and asked Kyleigh what she wanted to eat. She sat in the passenger's seat of the car and stared at the menu. "Mom, can you ask them how many carbs a burger and fries would have?" she asked. Kyleigh knew that food (specifically carbs) would make her blood sugar increase if she did not administer the correct amount of insulin with the food. She also knew that if she gave herself too much insulin because the carb count was not correct, her blood sugar could get dangerously low. The voice on the speaker asked if we were ready to order. I said, "Not quite, but can you tell us how many carbs are in the burger and fries?" The voice did not know so Kyleigh kept staring. Finally, Kyleigh settled on the salad and a water. I placed the order and we drove forward.

As I paid the person at the window, Kyleigh was busy pricking her finger to check her blood sugar. "Do you know how many carbs are in this salad?" I asked the employee. Again, they didn't know and Kyleigh began to panic. "What are we going to do, Mom?" she asked in a frightened voice. I told her not to worry and reminded her we had an app that could help us find out how many carbs were in this meal.

I took the salad and drink, pulled forward to park in an empty parking space, and took out my phone to find app. The app had a section for fast food, and I held my breath hoping that the restaurant we had picked would be there. I found the specific section, clicked on salads, and Voilà! The Apple Pecan Chicken salad with dressing was 52g of carbs. I let Kyleigh know the carb count and got ready to drive off. The interior light was on in the car and before I backed out of the parking place, I looked over at Kyleigh. She was sitting in the seat with the salad on her lap, tears hitting the lid.

Concerned, I quickly asked her what was wrong. In my mind, we had succeeded—we had food and figured out the carb count for the meal. Her crying got louder as she tried getting her supplies out of her bag to draw up a dose of insulin. I asked again.

This time she responded. "I hate math! Mom, it isn't the pain from pricks or needles that make me sad about diabetes, it is all the drama about food. I can't even eat a salad until I do a bazillion math problems and if I do the problem wrong,

I'm going to die. You know how much I stink at math." Now the tears flooded out of her eyes, and I felt the raw emotions of sadness mixed with anger.

Through my own tears, I attempted to comfort her and gave her some words of encouragement like, "You can do this! I know you can and just think about how this is going to improve your math skills." My words did not provide great solace probably because I, too, didn't really believe that diabetes was going to be the wonderful math tutor that Kyleigh needed. I understood her thoughts about diabetes. I was certain she hated it and thought it was an evil curse. The pain of being certain of my child's thoughts cut my heart like a sharp knife.

Kyleigh was never good at keeping her thoughts about her disease quiet. As a parent, I am grateful she shared her thoughts and feelings so we could talk about them and address them head on. About a year after being diagnosed with T1D, we were having a family dinner. I tried to give Kyleigh some autonomy with managing her diabetes and attempted to avoid hovering, but at dinner, I noticed she came to the table and put down her PDM (the tool that keeps track of her blood sugar and gives doses of insulin to her pump). I didn't see her do anything with her PDM, and she was eating. I thought it was odd because eating food meant her blood sugar would rise. She needed insulin with meals to help maintain her blood sugar, but she couldn't give the insulin unless she knew her blood sugar in the moment. I must have missed her pre-meal process. I didn't say anything and continued eating dinner with the kids, letting the question swirl in my head.

We finished dinner and I began cleaning up while the kids went back to homework. As I picked the dishes off the table, I noticed Kyleigh's PDM sitting on the table. I couldn't stop wondering how Kyleigh managed the insulin dose since I missed her finger stick. I decided to check. I picked up her PDM, pressed the buttons to the blood sugar history tab, and saw that the last recorded blood sugar was several days prior.

I thought I must be doing something wrong because Kyleigh had to check her blood sugar with every meal, but this didn't have the numbers from dinner or any of the prior meals from the week. I kept pressing buttons hoping I would find another screen. Nothing. Now panicked, I took a breath, hoping I was doing something wrong and called Kyleigh to help.

When Kyleigh appeared, I saw her face as I stood with her PDM in my hands. I immediately knew what I saw on the screen was true based on the guilty look on Kyleigh's face. My stomach sank. Kyleigh grabbed the PDM and got angry. "Don't touch my things!" she yelled. I told her I didn't understand what was happening.

Tears started flowing from Kyleigh's eyes like a faucet and she explained, "I just wanted to pretend like I didn't have diabetes anymore!"

Those words crushed my soul. I would do anything to take away this disease from my child! I knew there was nothing I could do to make it go away. As strongly as she no longer wanted diabetes, I felt one hundred times stronger about not wanting her to have diabetes.

When she said those words, I stopped and hugged her. I told her how much I loved her and wanted to take it away from her but couldn't. I told her we needed to accept checking sugars was part of life because she was killing herself if she didn't. We just stood there for a few minutes hugging as we both cried, wishing things were different. A little piece of my heart broke that day, longing for the days when Kyleigh was an infant and couldn't tell me what she was thinking. But as painful as her words were, I needed to hear them. Her words gave me perspective. It allowed me to support her with love and compassion. I could teach her that feeling sad or frustrated is OK, but our actions don't need to be fueled by those emotions. I was grateful for Kyleigh's heart wrenching thoughts because I could be a focused educator and help my child grow.

Learning About The Action And Result Of Maintaining Perspective Through My Patient

I needed perspective for my patients, too. When I was a young pediatric attending physician covering the inpatient ward, I had an incredible team of residents that helped care for our patients and learned about treatments as I supervised them. One of those patients was a young girl who was admitted because her physicians thought she was faking her symptoms. They had no good explanation for what was wrong with her. The young girl's father explained that the child began complaining of poor vision. Her school performance decreased because she couldn't see the board. The parents had taken her to an optometrist who couldn't find anything wrong with her vision.

Over the next several weeks, the child continued complaining of problems with her vision and told her parents her vision was getting worse. The parents returned to the eye doctor, but there still was no diagnosis made. The optometrist wondered if the child was stressed, and her physical symptoms were a manifestation of her emotional state. He recommended having her seen by a psychiatrist.

The parents were concerned about their daughter and followed the recommendation of the eye doctor. The psychiatrist did not find any source of trauma or stress at the initial visit but agreed that the child's symptoms could be malingering (exaggerating) if the eye specialists could not find a cause of the symptoms. The psychiatrist recommended a follow-up appointment.

As the parents waited for the follow-up, the child's symptoms continued progressing. She was now bumping into objects and claiming she couldn't see them. The parents decided to make an appointment with the child's pediatrician. At that visit, just like the other providers, the pediatrician couldn't determine a cause for the child's symptoms but knew closer monitoring might help lead to a diagnosis. The pediatrician recommended admission to the inpatient ward for close monitoring and further evaluation.

The child came to the pediatric ward with her parents, and I went into her room to hear her story and conduct my own exam. When I entered the room, there was a ten-year-old beautiful girl dressed in a hospital gown, returning to her bed from the restroom. I watched as she walked to her bed using her hands to feel before taking a step, similar to a blind person. I introduced myself and quietly observed her movements as she continued hesitantly shuffling through the room. The girl got into the bed as I spoke with her parents who were concerned and frustrated. They had watched their daughter deteriorate and no one could help. I spoke to the girl who begged me to believe her, because she was aware that everyone thought she was embellishing her symptoms. Hearing the perspective of my patients always helped me care for them. I stood and listened.

I left the room after completing my exam and knew that something was wrong with the patient. I listened to her and heard her parents' concerns. My gut told me this was not a correct diagnosis of malingering. I spoke to the residents on call that evening and asked them to keep a close eye on her. One of the residents was a neurology-trained pediatric resident. He was excited to see her after the evening check out was complete. He promised he would do a full physical exam and let me know his thoughts.

Later that evening, the resident called me and explained that the girl's physical exam findings were genuine. He had performed special neurological tests that he learned from his prior training in neurology. The test results were not normal and demonstrated cause for concern. He recommended we obtain an MRI. I agreed. He discussed the imaging study plan with the girl's parents, and the MRI was obtained overnight. The following morning, we had our diagnosis—multiple sclerosis. The MRI showed several areas of involvement, and treatment needed to begin immediately. MS medications can effectively resolve symptoms, but relapses might occur in the future.

The resident and I discussed the findings with the parents and child. I will never forget the relief they expressed with having a diagnosis. They were filled with emotions—anger at the previous physicians who thought their child was malingering, guilt because they didn't believe their child, concern over the new diagnosis, and gratitude for an answer. Recognizing their perspective allowed me to treat this patient with compassion and empathy. As I watched the parents verbally and physically express their emotions through tears, I knew they were becoming members of the club. Without practice, they understood the perspective of their child, but also allowed their child to witness their processing of emotions. They were going to be the exact supporters and role models this young girl needed.

Lessons About Maintaining Perspective

As parents, it is difficult to watch our children suffer. We want them to lead a happy life full of only beautiful experiences but having this goal for our children will not allow them to successfully maneuver the roller coaster ride. When we try to protect our children from experiencing any challenging emotions, we are setting them up for future failure. They will not be comfortable experiencing emotions such as fear, doubt, anxiety, or overwhelm so instead of processing emotion, they will resist emotion.

The struggles we face during our journey with a child with medical challenges is an opportunity for us to personally grow. It is also an opportunity for us to be teachers to our children. We can teach our children how to experience challenges and we can become role models on how to process emotions.

When Kyleigh was being treated for neuroblastoma, her screams and cries triggered my brain to question, *Why is this happening to me?* This thought creates a victim mentality which keeps us stuck in a state of sadness and fear. The ability to back up and take a broader perspective is an important action which can help us move forward. When we have a very myopic perspective, we become paralyzed with emotions when bad events happen to us. Changing our perspective to realize that lots of people experience bad things in the world can help us gain acceptance of the challenging parts of life.

When children have chronic conditions, parents have lots of "theys." I caught myself with thoughts around doctors, teachers, and family members as my "theys." Some examples of my thoughts included:

They aren't helping me.

They think I can do everything.

They have no idea what I go through in a day.

They treat us like a textbook, not a real person.

I was losing perspective, turning these individuals into villains, and feeling like I was their victim. I blamed them for the challenges I faced with my daughter, Kyleigh. It was their fault when I felt angry or disappointed.

The victim mentality is dangerous. It allows another individual to have power over you and takes away your emotional control. If you identify as a victim, this loss of emotional control can impact how you live in your life. It leads to hopelessness and negativity that often bleeds into other areas of your life.

When we feel miserable, our minds create villains by wanting it to be someone's fault. We eventually become trapped because we are in a constant loop of self-pity. We have placed our "they" in charge of how we feel. Often this loss of power occurs subconsciously so to stop the loop, we need to be aware that we are taking on a victim role. Blame, defensiveness, and complaining are clues that we are acting as victims.

All our feelings are created by our thinking. It is our responsibility to determine how we want to feel, even with unpleasant emotions. Processing negative emotions and intentionally choosing how we want to think about the people in our lives can build confidence and resiliency. It maintains our perspective of life.

Our ability to be happy does not come from the happiness of others. This is an important fact for parents to understand, since we often find ourselves trying to fix our children's unhappiness—thinking it will lead to our own personal happiness.

Here are ways to help maintain perspective.

1. **UNDERSTAND RESPONSIBILITY.** Our children's ability to be happy does not come from us. Everyone is responsible for their own emotions. As Kyleigh's mother, I was not going to make her happy about her diabetes. Her thoughts about wanting to pretend she didn't have diabetes were making her unhappy. My responsibility as a parent was teaching her how to appropriately manage her feelings about diabetes.

2. **BE A TEACHER.** We miss out on an opportunity to educate our children if we don't allow them to fully experience their emotions. I didn't want Kyleigh to hide the fact that she wasn't checking her blood sugars. Having open communication would have allowed me to teach her about her feelings rather than being surprised by her actions. These are difficult conversations but will pay dividends in the child's life.

3. **BE A ROLE MODEL.** It is OK for our children to be mad or scared if they are poked by nurses. It is OK for our children to be angry and frustrated when their diagnosis is not going away. This is our time to be a role model—by processing our own emotions and teaching our children to process theirs. The parents of my patient with multiple sclerosis allowed

their child to witness their tears. They processed an array of emotions when they learned her diagnosis. Modeling emotional control was a gift they gave to their child that will forever impact her life.

Our ability to choose our thoughts and avoid the victim role takes practice and consistency. We cannot expect perfection and sometimes we will lose perspective and fall back into the victim role. This is part of being human, but awareness brings understanding. With time and continued practice, maintaining our perspective can become our superpower.

Chapter 9

NEGLECT

> *"To keep a lamp burning, we have to keep putting oil in it." – Mother Teresa*

O ur priorities shift when we become a parent. Suddenly, we are responsible for a precious life and this responsibility can consume us. When we are faced with a new challenge that changes our current course of life, it is normal that our attention shifts and our priorities are disrupted. Adding a child's chronic diagnosis to parenthood can sadly, lead to discounting our competing priorities and creates harsh self-judgment. This ultimately results in neglect of self and others.

The words "should" and "should have" enter our vocabulary. The definition of *should* is "to indicate obligation, duty, or correctness, typically when criticizing someone's actions." This is a dangerous word when our brain uses it to obligate or criticize our own actions. Our brain uses this word to dictate what we need to be doing in the future, but it also uses it in the past tense to criticize our prior actions. We are left feeling guilty and ashamed. We begin to be consumed by these self-judgments and neglect living in the present. The "should" and "should have" thoughts generated leave us beating ourselves up and we forget to really live our lives.

Learning About The Action And Result Of Neglect Through Kyleigh

I always wanted a large family. My desire to become a mother was even stronger than my desire to become a physician. I was so grateful for the birth of Jake, my oldest son, and my heart felt like it would explode with gratitude when one child turned into two. I knew the parenting workload would increase, but I didn't fully appreciate how much work would be on my plate until after we brought Kyleigh home from the hospital and a toddler was waiting for my attention, too. I loved every minute of it. Even in the moments of absolute chaos, I reminded myself that these times were fleeting and I found joy. I knew that sooner than I wanted, the kids would no longer be little.

I was in residency when Kyleigh was born, and I had six weeks of maternity leave after her birth. I knew those six weeks would pass quickly, so I needed to maximize my time for being a "real mom." Jake, Kyleigh, and I did everything during those six weeks. I didn't have a stroller that fit both kids, so I put Jake in a backpack, strapped him to my back, and off we went with Kyleigh in the stroller. We blew bubbles in the park. We laughed at the animals at the zoo. We kicked the ball on the soccer fields. I knew Kyleigh would never remember these moments, but these activities would be important to Jake who was almost two years old at the time. I didn't want him to think that this new human creature I brought home had taken his mom. I wanted him to understand that it was fun to have a sister.

I returned to work and continued my fun moments with the kids when my schedule allowed, but all this fun came to a screeching halt a few months later when Kyleigh was diagnosed with neuroblastoma.

When we were given Kyleigh's diagnosis, my very full plate immediately began overflowing. Kyleigh required lots of attention with the countless daily diaper and outfit changes due to chemo-induced diarrhea, daily central line dressing changes and line flushing, and evening nasogastric tube placements. Neuroblastoma robbed Kyleigh of her infancy, but it also robbed Jake of his mom's attention.

Mother-son playdates of enjoying bubbles became Jake observing me flush Kyleigh's central line. One day as I was flushing Kyleigh's central line, the fluid immediately leaked from the wound site. The line had become dislodged and non-functional. I immediately knew this meant another trip to the operating room to replace the central line. "Shit!" I yelled in frustration. Jake spontaneously repeated, "Sit, momma! Sit!" That innocent repetition of curse words reminded me that my beautiful two-year-old child used to say, "Pop, momma! Pop!" during the bubble blowing moments that were now a distant memory. An incredible sadness overtook me along with an intense desire to go back to the way things were prior to Kyleigh's diagnosis.

Jake was an innocent victim of neuroblastoma as much as Kyleigh. Jake didn't experience the physical impact of the disease like Kyleigh, but the neglect he experienced undoubtedly had an emotional impact. I did the best I could with what I knew at the time, but I would do things differently if I could turn back the hands of time. Throughout Jake's childhood, he challenged me as a parent, and I often wondered if this was trying to get my attention. Would things have been different if I made more time to blow bubbles with him when Kyleigh was sick?

The world stopped again when Kyleigh was diagnosed with diabetes. All my physical and emotional focus was trying to get my twelve-year-old daughter adjusted to her diagnosis. When she went back to school after her inpatient admission, I went with her. She danced ballet and attended a school for the arts, which made me more nervous because I knew the challenges that were involved in managing blood sugars during intense physical activity. I sat outside of her class and watched through a window. I hoped my presence would provide Kyleigh some comfort, knowing I was there to help, but I was also there to cheer. I wanted her to understand this new diagnosis would not be something that held her back from her dreams. She could do anything, even if this new medical issue was functioning as an obstacle during this time in her life.

I missed work to watch over her. I rescheduled my clinic patients so I could attend her follow-up appointments. I slept poorly and further disrupted my poor sleep to go prick her finger and check her blood sugar in the middle of the night to make sure her evening dose of insulin had not caused her blood sugar to drop too low. Kyleigh was diagnosed with diabetes in September and set a goal to have an insulin pump by Thanksgiving to minimize the pokes. She knew her doctors weren't going to prescribe a pump until she understood more about diabetes and how to manage blood sugars. My goal was to get a continuous glucose monitor (CGM) so I would have a better idea of her blood sugars. Kyleigh met her ambitious goal, but my goal took longer to obtain because it would be too overwhelming to be prescribed two devices that she would always need to have attached to her. The pump was the priority. I continued monitoring her blood sugars by scrolling through her meter and waking at night. I told myself things would get better after the CGM.

Kyleigh was ready for a CGM about one year after her diagnosis. When we got it, I found out I was wrong to think this device would help me get my life back. The CGM fed into an app on my phone. If Kyleigh's blood sugar was low, it alerted me. If Kyleigh's blood sugar was high, it alerted me. The app even alerted if Kyleigh did not have the CGM in place. Kyleigh began referring to me as her "diabetic helicopter mom."

Kyleigh was diagnosed with diabetes when her youngest brother was five years old. My awareness of how I thought I neglected Jake when she had neuroblastoma made me work to prevent this from recurring with Jake and now Tyler, my third child. I made sure they each had equal consumption of my attention and even started "Mommy Dates" for special focused attention. I understand now that this was at my own expense. I neglected myself.

My actions after Kyleigh's diagnosis forced me to neglect my career, my health, and my sleep. I again became an overwhelmed shell of myself—like when she was receiving chemotherapy years earlier. I once again struggled with feelings of guilt about the neglect, but this time I was neglecting myself. I then felt guilty over feeling selfish for wanting to take care of myself. This led to even more neglect and the cycle continued.

Learning About The Action And Result Of Neglect Through My Patient

As a doctor, I taught patients, but I also learned countless things from speaking to and observing my patients and their families. It has been a privilege to be both teacher and student. I had the privilege of caring for a beautiful girl who had many medical issues. Ally was about ten years old and had significant cerebral palsy and developmental delay. She was nonverbal with a tracheostomy tube to help her breath, and her family used a wheelchair to transport her. Ally had lots of medical challenges, including seizures and problems with her urinary tract, but these were managed well by her mother. Ally was well-loved by her family.

Ally couldn't eat any food because the food would go into her lungs (aspiration), so she received her nutrition through a feeding tube. But Ally loved lollipops. Every time she saw me and needed to get a blood draw, her mom brought a lollipop for a reward. After the blood draw, I would see Ally laying on the exam table with her mom letting her lick a red lollipop. The secretions from Ally's tracheostomy tube would soon become red, matching the red-tinged secretions in her mouth.

One day, Ally was admitted with pneumonia, and I went to see her on the pediatric ward. Ally's mother was sitting there, and her body language was tense. I asked if everything was OK. She explained that the inpatient physicians had just come in and told her she should never have given Ally lollipops. The physicians told her the lollipops were the cause of Ally's pneumonia. I sat down, seeing that Ally's mom needed to vent.

As I listened, Ally's mother explained to me that caring for her daughter was hard. Because of Ally's developmental delays, she only smiled periodically and never laughed, but Ally's mom knew that the lollipops brought Ally joy. She told me she learned many years ago that things were going to happen to Ally and not everything would be in her control, but she could control bringing her daughter joy. She explained that Ally got pneumonia in the past—with and without lollipops. In our conversation, she was adamant that the lollipops were going to continue.

She then said something I have never forgotten. "I gave up blaming myself long ago. If I listened to people that told me, 'You should have . . .,' I would feel guilty every day and neglect the things that bring us joy. I stopped listening to that noise a long time ago."

Ally's pneumonia got better and I continued to see Ally and her mom in clinic. Her mom learned to practice doing joyous things for herself, her child, and her family by drowning out the self-judgment. This gave her confidence to choose her actions. I am grateful for the wisdom she shared with me that day. I occasionally catch myself saying "should" or "should have" and it reminds me of the conversation in Ally's hospital room. In those moments, I take the advice of Ally's mom and stop listening. This is freeing. We can suck on a lollipop without regret.

Lessons On Neglect

As a pediatrician, I often observed parents becoming consumed by parenthood, leading to forgetting who they are as individuals. This act of neglecting ourselves and our relationships is even more frequent in parents with chronically ill children.

Our thoughts about our situation will not always be pleasant, but they are always the driving force behind our feelings and actions. Feeling overwhelmed with emotions such as sadness, despair, or pain will result in neglect. We may choose to be alone or stay in bed, avoiding the world around us. While it's understandable to want to retreat in these moments, it's important to remember that pain is part of life, and everyone experiences it at some point. What makes us human is our ability to feel both joy and pain. If we can learn to process emotions during difficult moments in life and grow from the experience, we will become stronger versions of ourselves.

Chronic illness takes a toll on everyone in the family, but it can be especially difficult for parents. The constant worry and stress of caring for a sick child can lead to neglecting our own needs. We may not have time for hobbies or friends, and our relationship with our partner can suffer. It's important to remember that taking care of ourselves is not selfish, but rather it's necessary to be the best possible parent for our child.

The moment Kyleigh was diagnosed with diabetes, life changed. From that point forward, life was filled with thoughts of insulin and carbs. My days were filled with checking her blood sugar numbers on her glucose monitor app because I never let go of managing Kyleigh's diabetes. I never fully trusted Kyleigh's school, and my days were filled with emailing, calling, and meeting her teachers. I was worried about her nutrition, so I spent time planning meals and counting carbs. I was working full-time as a physician, but I was distracted with Kyleigh's medical visits and trips to the pharmacy. Uninterrupted nights of sleep were impossible. I felt a deep sadness and a profound sense of worry. I tried to limp along like an athlete who was ignoring an injury. In retrospect, I was bad at diagnosing my pain because doing so meant admitting something was wrong. I felt like admitting pain was admitting weakness. I wanted to brush it off before someone noticed I was injured. Instead of diagnosing it, my pain festered. I neglected my life.

We shouldn't live in a state of emptiness like I experienced. My life was not balanced. I needed time for myself and time for my other children. I needed time for relationships with a significant other, family, and friends. I needed time for career goals.

It is amazing how organization and planning can change everything! Our time is valuable, and our use of time helps us create balance and achieve goals. We can't add hours to the day, but we can maximize our use of time. I learned how to organize time on a calendar, ensuring my use of time is in line with my priorities. This organizational tool has been a valuable resource for achieving goals, eliminating unproductive "breaks," and decreasing neglect.

Being a parent of a child with a medical diagnosis adds tasks to my day, but time management allows me to govern these tasks and accomplish the other commitments I make to myself and others. I transformed my chaotic, numb life into an organized, priority-focused, vibrant existence.

I cared for too many children at the hospital whose parents are just trying to hang on. The parents bounce from one appointment to the next, just like a pinball, and become consumed with their child while forgetting to live intentionally. A pinball sometimes lands on the magic spot and lots of points are acquired, but other times the ball is knocked around by the flippers and eventually slips through the slot, losing the turn. The pinball has no strategy. It aimlessly bounces around the playfield. When we get overwhelmed with life, we bounce like a pinball and neglect creating goals.

There are three steps to making any goal happen.

1. **BELIEVE.** A goal starts with a dream that develops into a deep-seated belief. This belief may be held by only you. For a goal to come true, only you need to believe it can happen. The belief is very specific and can be described with great detail. Putting a time constraint on a goal gives our belief even more specificity. Ally's mom believed in her goal to bring her daughter joy.

2. **COMMIT.** To achieve a goal, you need an unwavering commitment to make it happen. The roadmap doesn't need to be clear, but you must be able to maintain your inner belief that you will get there when things are easy *and* when things are hard. People who don't reach their goal didn't commit to the belief and when the going got tough, they gave up. Ally's mom was committed to her plan for giving Ally a lollipop if she underwent a painful procedure. She understood the risks but believed strongly in her desire to bring joy to Ally.

3. **PLAN TO FAIL.** To reach a goal, you must continue to take steps. Expect, though, that failure will happen. These are opportunities to learn and should be welcomed, not avoided. When setting a goal, we may not be able to fully map out the plan to get us there, but if we start, we can continue to rely on our commitment to determine the next step to try. The doctors tried to convince Ally's mom that she failed with her simple lollipop goal. Having a

strong commitment to the goal gave Ally's mom the courage to disagree during the hospital admission.

Parents worry about their children. Parents with a child with a chronic condition worry even more. However, when we start neglecting ourselves and others, we stop living. Thriving in life is exactly what our children need. Parents can do a better job of caring for their child when they feel complete and full. In addition, children need parents who accomplish goals so that they can learn anything is possible. They build confidence by watching their confident parents.

Chapter 10

CELEBRATIONS

"The more you praise and celebrate your life, the more there is in life to celebrate." – Oprah Winfrey

---

C elebrating is an underrated skill. Most people don't take time to celebrate meaningful actions or events in their lives. Celebrations help people stay motivated and create momentum. Without celebrations will we lose our drive to succeed.

Learning About The Action And Result Of Celebrations Through Kyleigh

Kyleigh's first year of neuroblastoma treatment was filled with highs and devastating lows. I had tremendous personal growth during that year and finished the year with a sense of gratitude. I was grateful for the medical treatment available for her. I was grateful for the love and support of family and friends. I was grateful for the life of my child.

Kyleigh's first birthday happened about a month after her last dose of chemo. She was skinnier than ideal, and we continued to manage profuse diarrhea resulting from surgery and chemotherapy. Overall, she was doing great. She had no central line in place. She was eating well and no longer required the NG tube feedings at night. She was walking and even putting two words together in a sentence. We continued struggling with intense separation anxiety, but I hoped things would improve with time. It was time for a celebration!

Despite having returned to work, I planned a party. I wanted to thank the medical staff who provide exceptional care to Kyleigh during the year and celebrate her life with family and friends. My real motivation, though, was to feel normal. I loved being a mom and I always felt I was put on earth with this as my mission. I enjoyed being pregnant with both Jake and Kyleigh. It was an honor to have a life grow inside me and feel it move and kick. I loved moments in Jake's infancy, and the camera was never far from reach to capture life's precious moments.

Kyleigh's infancy, however, was ripped away from me. Rides in strollers were through the hallways of a hospital instead of the neighborhood sidewalks. Rocking to sleep became a necessity for comfort after an NG tube was placed. This party was my way of showing myself that life could return to normal.

I invited tons of people—her doctors, her doctors' families, our colleagues and friends, our family. No one was excluded from the celebration. I booked an outdoor party pavilion that had a grill and picnic tables and an area for volleyball and basketball. I instructed everyone that in lieu of gifts, they should bring an unwrapped toy for any age child for donation to the Pediatric Hematology/Oncology clinic. We had tons of food including hamburgers, hotdogs, food trays of fruits and vegetables, and a huge cake.

On the day of the party, we arrived early to set up the food and balloons. We had a plastic bin decorated with the words "Treasure Chest" where everyone could place their donated gifts. It looked perfect. Before attendees arrived, I decided to put sunscreen on Jake and Kyleigh. I did Jake first and quickly rubbed in the thick lotion on his pale white skin. Kyleigh was next. I rubbed the lotion over her bald little head and on her face and neck before moving to her little arms and legs. She began crying and I assumed it was because I was trying to keep her still while applying the sunscreen.

When I was done with the application process, I put her down and set her free. The crying continued. I saw she was rubbing her eyes. As she did so, the crying got louder and she stood still trying to open her eyes, but it was too painful to do so. I got sunscreen in her eyes, and I realized she was making it worse because her hands were covered with sunscreen. Each time she tried to rub her eyes, her eyes became more painful as the sunscreen came off her hands and into her eyes. As I looked at Kyleigh and understood what happened, I panicked. I had just ruined her party with sunscreen.

I picked her up and raced to the bathroom. Maybe I could rinse her eyes and save the celebration. Kyleigh cried as I tried to hold her head over the sink and prevent her from making things worse by rubbing her eyes. I stood with the water running, attempting to use my hands to rinse away the misplaced sunscreen as tears rolled down my cheeks. What had I done?

I did the best I could at the sink. I rinsed her hands and eyes, but her eyes were now bright red and the skin around her eyes was irritated. Thankfully she had stopped crying and seemed to feel better. I placed Kyleigh down and looked at the mirror for a moment, seeing the tired reflection that appeared. I then realized this was exactly what I wanted. I wanted a party that would help me feel normal again. I wanted a day to not have chemo or central lines or mortality rates creep into my brain. This was exactly that. I got to spend the day worrying about sunscreen in Kyleigh's eyes rather than worrying about if the chemotherapy was able to destroy any remaining cancer cells. I happily took this little hiccup that "normal" parents get to worry about. This was my "normal" day. I wiped my face and with a smile, walked with Kyleigh out of the bathroom.

The party was perfect, sunscreen mishap and all. We shared stories and laughs and had the opportunity to thank those involved in Kyleigh's care. Everyone had full bellies and we had hearts full of gratitude. We cleaned up the leftovers and loaded the car after the full day, including Kyleigh's favorite balloon and two huge bins full of toys for the oncology kids. The day flew by, but the previous year taught me to embrace these fleeting moments and celebrate the moments life gives you—especially the "normal" ones.

Years later, when Kyleigh was twelve, she had learned a great deal about service dogs by completing the volunteer project involving Archie, the hospital therapy dog, months prior to her diagnosis of diabetes. She learned the difference between a service dog and a therapy dog. She learned about training techniques and the joy these dogs brought their owners and the patients at the hospital. Kyleigh was obsessed with these gifted animals.

When Kyleigh was diagnosed with diabetes, Archie came to visit in her hospital room. After the visit, Kyleigh asked if she could get a diabetic alert dog now that she had diabetes. Without blinking an eye, I adamantly said no to her request. We had not even left the hospital yet! We needed to get comfortable with our new life so now was not the time to add the additional stress of caring for an animal. I was 100 percent comfortable denying this request, plus we already had two dogs at home.

Three years passed after her service project and diabetes diagnosis. During that time, a lot changed and sadly, both our dogs died. We grieved the loss of our greyhounds who, ironically, both passed away from bone cancer almost one year apart. Our house was quieter without our four-legged family members, and the kids missed their furry friends. Kyleigh was adjusting to life with diabetes, but I was sure I would never say she had "adjusted."

One day, Kyleigh was scrolling on social media and saw an ad for diabetic alert dogs. The service dog organization's website explained that they were given a grant to give away one free diabetic alert dog. When Kyleigh told me, I thought there must be a catch. Through the years Kyleigh had not stopped asking for a service dog. She asked many times, and sometimes I quietly did a little research on the animals to provide evidence that my "no" was still the correct parental decision. I learned through my googling that diabetic alert dogs are close to $25K! These are expensive animals, and my scientific doctor brain was not convinced they were really able to alert for blood sugar swings.

Kyleigh read more about the service dog grant and understood there was a selection process which required an extensive application. Kyleigh downloaded the application and began to work. This application was more challenging than any college application I had ever seen. She poured her heart and soul into essay after essay and clearly demonstrated she was motivated to receive a diabetic alert dog. I did a little research on my own and knew it was legitimate. I let her proceed expelling her energy on the application process because I had no problem with the gift if Kyleigh was selected. Even if the dog didn't alert, I knew it would be a well-trained dog and would not require a large financial investment. Kyleigh took time writing, editing, and re-editing her essays, but after a few days, she hit the submit button.

About two months later, my cell phone rang. It was the CEO of the service dog organization calling to tell me that Kyleigh was selected to be the recipient of a free diabetic alert dog. My emotions overcame me in that moment. I was overjoyed with excitement and gratitude. I began crying and explained that Kyleigh seemed to have bad luck, but this was a sign that her luck was turning. I knew how excited Kyleigh would be when I told her the news. I was right on that prediction, and when I called Kyleigh, she joined me in tears of joy.

We waited for months after that call to have Kyleigh's diabetic alert dog delivered to our house. Kyleigh chose the name Hazel after a character in her favorite movie, *The Fault in our Stars*. I found the name appropriate since the movie character was a patient with a pediatric cancer. It seemed that the name of this new dog was bringing together two worlds for Kyleigh—her former cancer world and her current diabetic world. We all did tasks to prepare for Hazel's homecoming.

On the day Hazel arrived, there was a flurry of activity at the house. I hired a photographer because I wanted someone to capture the moment Kyleigh and Hazel first met. A local news crew came to the house to do a story on diabetic alert dogs. We were dressed and ready for pictures and cameras. When the trainer pulled up, the excitement from everyone was palpable. We walked outside to meet the newest member of our family.

The trainer got out of the car and introduced herself. As she walked to the back of the car, she asked Kyleigh if she was ready to meet Hazel. Kyleigh was staring and smiling like a child waiting for Santa to pull a present out of his bag. The trainer opened the door and the most beautiful black lab jumped out of the car. I know Kyleigh wanted to run and squeeze that dog, but she held back to make sure Hazel felt safe. Kyleigh gave Hazel a couple of pats on the head and then sat on the steps to get to eye level with her. The rest of us stood back and just watched the beginning of an incredible bond between this beautiful young human and adorable stunning dog.

After a minute or two, Hazel pawed Kyleigh's leg. I assumed was because the dog was enjoying Kyleigh's attention and wanted more petting. The trainer immediately said, "Kyleigh, she is alerting you. Do you have your meter?" I ran inside to get the supplies for Kyleigh to check her blood sugar and handed them to Kyleigh a minute later. Kyleigh pricked and checked. Her blood sugar was high. I wasn't surprised with the number—the excitement of the morning was probably the culprit for being out of range—but I was shocked that this dog really knew her blood sugar was off.

I referred to her as Hazel the Hero, and she was filled with a magical ability to bring joy to Kyleigh and help her manage a stinky disease. The day of Hazel's homecoming was a celebration. We celebrated the arrival of a tool to help manage good health, but we also celebrated this beautiful, loving creature that once again filled our house with joy.

Learning About The Action And Result Of Celebrations Through My Patient

Celebrations come in all shapes and sizes, but when caring for a chronically ill child, celebrations should never be missed. Even good-byes can be a time to celebrate. I met Brayden when he was about six months old and after seventeen years, came the last day I was going to be his doctor. It was a celebration of how far he had come.

Brayden was diagnosed with a serious and rare immunodeficiency called severe combined immunodeficiency (SCID). This condition prevents a person from fighting even a simple infection and can lead to death in infancy if untreated. He wasn't even born yet when his parents and physicians planned the medical journey that faced him after birth. He was born a few months later and admitted to the Neonatal Intensive Care Unit where the diagnosis was confirmed. Soon, he was transferred to Duke Medical Center and underwent the necessary treatment— bone marrow transplant. The days at Duke waiting for the transplant and then recovering from the transplant were challenging, but I didn't play a role in that part of Brayden's journey.

Brayden's parents brought him home when he was around six months old, and they brought him to my office to continue his care. Brayden was beautiful and happy. He did not appear sickly, but instead was bald and cherubic. His parents and I wore hospital gowns and masks because his immune system had not fully recovered, but other than our odd attire, the visit was similar to any other routine pediatric visit.

I reviewed the paperwork from Duke and the discharge summary. Brayden did remarkably well after the transplant, but his B cells did not regenerate. That meant Brayden's immune system was better than the one he was born with but still was compromised. He needed replacement antibody infusions for life. He started on these infusions before discharge from Duke and he would continue these infusions weekly.

Over the next seventeen years, I had the honor and privilege to watch Brayden grow. He changed from a cherubic baby to a chatty toddler to a fearless young child to a thoughtful, smart teenager. I helped him stay healthy and took care of him when he wasn't. I worked alongside his parents to ensure he received his weekly infusions, and I was supportive when Brayden was depressed because of his disease. The day of our last visit was the day I had to pass control to another physician and hope they would enjoy caring for him as much as I had.

We finished our last visit with me making sure Brayden understood his disease and encouraging him to be brave when independently administering his necessary weekly infusions. As we stood to say good-bye, I paused and took a hospital coin out of my pocket. I told him that before he and his family moved, I wanted to make sure he had something to remember the place that cared for him for so long. I explained that in WWI, an officer led an aviation unit and had coins made with their unit symbol. He told his soldiers to carry the coin with them on missions. One soldier later was shot down during a mission and used the coin to show the French soldiers that he was their ally. I told Brayden that today, soldiers are given coins when they perform honorably. If they are ever seen in a bar by their commander, the commander can ask to see their coin. If the soldier doesn't have possession of the coin at the time, the soldier has to buy the commander a beer!

I told Brayden that he was currently too young to drink, but if I see him in a bar later in life, he better be carrying his coin or else he is buying the beer. We all laughed. I then told him how much I enjoyed being his physician. I was privileged to learn a lot about medicine from him and he not only taught me, but I also used his story to teach other physicians about his immunodeficiency. Brayden gave me a hug and I told him this visit was not good-bye, but rather a see-you-later celebration. Brayden, his parents, and I stood in my office celebrating the journey we took together. We celebrated the hard work his parents did caring for Brayden, and we celebrated Brayden for keeping us on our toes, but always being strong. Celebrations are an important part of life and should never be missed. This small celebration in my office ended with a hug, handshake, and an exchange of the coin to its new owner. My heart was full. That evening I received a text from Brayden's parents. They understand the significance of this little celebration. They, too, were full of gratitude.

Lessons On Celebrations

The brain is like a young child. It requires supervision, avoids pain, and seeks pleasure. As a former pediatrician, I gave immunizations to many children. Afterward, they got a sticker. The tears from the shot were quickly replaced by a smile with the sticker. There were times, though, that our clinic ran out of stickers. The tears from the shot became tantrums, and the next shot was going to be more challenging. Our brains are the same as the small, sticker-loving child. Rewards keep the brain motivated. Without celebrations, our brains give up and we feel constantly defeated.

Celebrations also force our brains to focus on positive things. For example, planning a party causes the brain to focus on balloons, cakes, and the invitation list rather than finding evidence for our negative thoughts. When I threw Kyleigh her party after chemotherapy, I created the "Treasure Box" for guests to donate gifts so the tears of pediatric cancer patients could be replaced by smiles from the prizes out of the box. On the day of the event, I watched guest after guest place their donations in the box. My heart was exploding because I was focused on the positive—the joy would we bring future patients. There were no negative thoughts about challenging surgeries or neutropenic fevers, only positive thoughts of appreciation.

Birthday parties became our way to celebrate the future. As we sing "Happy Birthday," we are celebrating the past, but as the birthday person blows out the candles and makes a wish, we are celebrating their future. When we celebrate our personal future, we will generate positive motivation to continue creating extraordinary value in this world.

Here are areas to celebrate.

1. CELEBRATE YOURSELF. We want to become the best version of ourselves. Taking a moment to pause and ask what you learned through a specific experience can help you recognize and acknowledge your gifts and talents to celebrate yourself. Reflecting on the personal qualities needed to reach a goal can stir up good feelings of celebrating a victory. This can improve your confidence, sense of well-being, and satisfaction with life. During Kyleigh's birthday party, I had a moment in the mirror before leaving the bathroom after trying to wash the sunscreen out of Kyleigh's eyes. As I looked in the mirror, the reflection that looked back it me demonstrated

strength and resiliency. I had courageously climbed the mountains of chemotherapy with my daughter, and it was time to acknowledge victory.

2. **CELEBRATE YOUR ACCOMPLISHMENTS.** Celebrating your accomplishments creates motivation to continue to work toward future goals. If you accomplished something you never did before, celebrate. Your accomplishments always matter but focusing your thoughts on why your accomplishments matter leads to positive emotions to keep you thriving. We are inherently altruistic beings so reflecting on how our accomplishments impacted others will help to maintain our momentum. Hazel was a blessing because she would provide Kyleigh help with managing her blood sugar, but getting Hazel was also a time to celebrate Kyleigh's commitment to health. As a young teen, Kyleigh understood and managed a complicated medical diagnosis. Her accomplishments deserved celebration.

3. **CELEBRATE OTHERS.** Celebrating others demonstrates appreciation and reinforces positive behaviors. We need others so we grow into the best version of ourselves, and acknowledging the assistance of others can spread kindness. Spending time being grateful for others creates a contagious desire to do more in the world. I celebrated Brayden during our last visit in clinic because I wanted him to know how much I appreciated him. He helped me become a better doctor by challenging me with his medical condition. My celebration of him was

contagious. A few days later, I received a large envelope in the mail. It was a note and mountain bike race coin. Brayden was an avid bike racer, and he received the coin as an award during one of his races. The note was thanking me for being his doctor.

Being a parent of a chronically ill child is hard. Taking breaks to celebrate is not only helpful, but necessary. Celebrations can reflect our courage. We weren't given a choice to be a parent of a child with medical needs or a chronic illness, but we made the decision to positively contribute to the world. We overcome fear and do things we are afraid to do by using courage. Celebrations don't mean that we are perfect, but it does mean that we accept who we are. As parents, we are tough and scared, but we love our children and are committed to give them an extraordinary life. We will celebrate!

Chapter 11

GRATITUDE

> *"When we focus on gratitude, the tide of disappointment goes out and the tide of love rushes in."*
> *– Kristin Armstrong*

G ratitude is a powerful skill when we feel stuck in our lives. We can cultivate abundance by being grateful for our families, friends, the love in our lives, and the work that we do. When we see the silver lining in all our difficult situations and feel grateful for the opportunity to learn, we feel abundant. When we begin to feel more abundant, we then begin to attract a flow of abundance in our lives. It is a fact that what we choose to focus on grows. We can increase the abundance in life by focusing on all that we have.

Learning Gratitude Through Kyleigh

When I was a pediatric resident, my beautiful six-month-old baby girl was diagnosed with neuroblastoma. The diagnosis was a shock! I knew what it meant, and I knew the treatment path was going to be challenging. It was challenging. I learned a tremendous amount through the experience. I learned about resilience, communication, and teamwork. I am grateful I had the experience to build these skills. Thankfully, my daughter does not remember that time.

At the age of two, she fell in love with ballet. She danced intensely for years and danced pointe at the age of nine. She attended a school for the arts for ballet during middle school and part of high school. She was an amazing ballerina! When she was twelve, I stood in the bathroom of her ballet school, tested her urine, and through tears told my daughter she had diabetes. Diabetes changed everything. Her hardcore ballet teachers would kick her out of class if she wore her insulin pump. She struggled to keep her blood sugar up during her intense workouts. I watched as my beautiful ballerina's self-esteem crumbled. She transferred from the school and discovered ice hockey. The grace she demonstrated in the dance studio turned into skills on the ice, and she became a fierce ice hockey player.

She went on to attend honors college at the College of Charleston and graduated college at the age of nineteen, just three years after starting. She graduated with a 3.9999 GPA (she got an A- in a dance class that I wouldn't let her audit). She said goodbye to her life in South Carolina and began a new life in New Jersey where she attends Rutgers New Jersey School of Medicine as an MD/PhD student. She wants to understand autoimmunity. She wants to change the world, and I have no doubt she will.

Kyleigh is now twenty-two, has finished her first two years of medical school, passed Step 1 of the medical licensing exam, and is studying T-cells in an immunology lab. She owns a house and is engaged to be married next year. Her story has a happy ending, but the road to get there has been full of twists, turns, and bumps. I hated each obstacle, but I appreciate the opportunity we had to tackle each one. Through each experience, my daughter has grown into the incredible young woman she is today and loves the life she was given.

I am very proud of my daughter, but I share her stories because as I reflect on my young infant who beat neuroblastoma and now lives everyday with type 1 diabetes, I am inspired. Her strength and resilience are commendable. I am grateful to be her mother because she taught me that there is no goal too audacious to accomplish. Set your goals, write them down, work hard, and surpass each of them.

The hard work of doctors and nurses in medicine saved my daughter's life more than once. We all have the ability to make a difference in the lives of people around us. I am grateful for my daughter's experiences that reinforced this responsibility in my life.

Learning Gratitude Through My Life As A Physician

I have had an incredible career as a physician. As a small child, I dreamed of being able to care for children, but I have been able to do that and so much more. I have cared for angelic newborn babies and grouchy teenagers. I have sat with my elderly patient as she showed me gravesite pictures of the husband that she so desperately missed. I have cared for injured active duty service members who were protecting our freedom overseas. It has been an honor to care for each patient.

I'm grateful for my childhood, too. A very fond memory was when I was about six years old and we visited my grandparents in Dover, Delaware. My grandfather, a career Air Force non-commissioned officer and avid golfer, put a metal bucket on its side and took on the task of teaching my siblings and I how to putt. If we could hit the ball in the bucket, we got a nickel. After several attempts, I took my time. I took a deep breath. I pulled the club back, hit the ball, and prayed. There was immediate cheering when I got the ball in the bucket. A nickel was placed in my hand, and I felt like I was holding ten million dollars. I relived this moment many, many times throughout my life. It meant so much more to me than a ball, a bucket, and a nickel.

Pop-pop was my grandfather, and he was an important man in my life. He emigrated from Italy as a child but loved our country so much that he spent his career in the Air Force. I hated the moment a 21-gun salute was complete, and he was laid to rest in Section 67 of Arlington National Cemetery. Visiting his gravesite has given me peace through the years.

As I reflect on Pop-pop's golf lesson, his pride taught me a lot. Pop-pop was proud of all his grandkids. He loved us all. I like being an Army doctor, but I have loved being a mother. I am grateful and proud I was chosen to be a mother to my children. They are my inspiration.

Pop-pop was a great teacher and mentor. He cheered for me in my childhood golf lesson just as loudly as I screamed when my ball went in the bucket. I am grateful today to have a personal cheering section. Thankfully I had people swoop into my life and become my best friend and cheerleader. Golf isn't usually a team sport, but the game of life is. Be thankful for your teammates.

My childhood golf memory with my grandfather wasn't the first time I held a golf club. My parents introduced me to many things in life, including golf. They are responsible for my knowledge of hard work and dedication. Their example made me a better person. Appreciate your parents because through their perfect and imperfect times being a parent, they taught life lessons that made you into the human you are today.

I wasn't a natural golfer. The ball didn't go in the bucket on my first attempt or second attempt or third attempt. I continued to swing and with each golf stroke, I got closer and closer to the bucket. Sometimes life isn't a perfect putting green. There are divots that put your ball in places you didn't anticipate. I certainly experienced my fair share of divots, but I'm thankful for my village that rallied behind me. Take time to be grateful to those who shared their time, energy, and love with you.

Jack Nicklaus was a superstar to my grandfather. To my grandfather's chagrin, I did not become an avid golfer, so I never really idealized golfers like Tiger Woods. I do have superstars in my life, though. My mentors taught me to be the physician, teacher, and leader that I am today. Be grateful for your mentors.

When I finally got the ball in the bucket during my grandfather's game, he gave me a nickel. Five little cents, but to me it felt like millions. Today, I am surrounded by million-dollar nickels. Throughout my career, I trained thousands of medical students, interns, residents, and fellows. I have cared for countless patients. I worked with amazing nurses and administrators who made my life easier. I am honored to be given the opportunity to teach, and I am humbled to be given the responsibility to care for military members and their families. Each of these people are a million-dollar nickels in my world.

I entered the medical field with an inherent desire to help people. I am grateful I have been able to do this, but as I reflect on my experiences, I know I can do more. I am grateful for the mind I was given to help teach patients about their disease. I am grateful for the skills to mentor young physicians who can help even more patients. I am grateful for the opportunity to continue to help future individuals.

Lessons On Gratitude

We can create more joy through the loving expression of gratitude. As we focus on love, we indeed create more of that, and love is core and central to all manifestation in our lives. When we create from a place of love and intention, our lives become joyous and rich. Gratitude can start a positive momentum in your life. When you begin having an "attitude of gratitude" in your life, you jump-start the process of manifesting the life you want to create.

Here are actions that develop the skill of gratitude:

1. **APPRECIATE WHAT YOU ALREADY HAVE.** Look for what you want to see versus what you don't want to see. Too often we go about our day waiting and expecting awful things to happen or expecting to be disappointed. We walk around saying, "I don't like this," and look for things that need changing. You will find that your world may be more to your liking if you focus on what you do want to see. "I like this, and I really love that!" This can

shift from a negative to a positive focus in your brain. When Kyleigh's self-esteem plummeted from being wrongfully treated in ballet class after her diabetes diagnosis, I could have thought, "I don't like ballet." I instead chose to think about how I appreciated ballet and the opportunity it gave my daughter. It taught her about hard work and commitment, values every parent wishes to instill in their child.

2. **APPRECIATE SOMETHING ABOUT YOURSELF.** The biggest gift we can ever give is unconditional love of ourselves. If we love ourselves no matter what, we can set big goals and take risks to reach them without the fear of failure. We are always worthy and don't need to rely on anyone else to generate our confidence. We look inside. Worthiness is accepting ourselves exactly how we are without comparing to others. A positive self-perception with unconditional love builds our belief of worthiness. Worthiness becomes our shield as we go through the challenges of life. I am a great mother, but I am not perfect. I have been critical to my kids about their hair, clothing, or choice of makeup. I appreciate that I have self-awareness and can grow from these mistakes.

3. **APPRECIATE THE WORLD AROUND YOU.** Look for beauty in your life such as the snow, leaves, and sun. Focus on the nickel you have instead of the one you don't. I am so grateful for my career as a physician. Every patient that sat on my exam table taught me a lesson. Sometimes it was a lesson about

medicine, other times it was a lesson about life, but I remain grateful for it all.

There are so many emotions that each of us is able to experience. Some emotions feel amazing such as joy, love, excitement, confidence, and pride. Some emotions feel uncomfortable such as sadness, frustration, anger, doubt, and overwhelm. Feelings are what make life vibrant and wonderful, but the vividness of life is only possible with experiencing both amazing and uncomfortable emotions. We need to be grateful for both.

Think of feelings as an array of colors. If you were to assign each feeling a color, it becomes clear that all are needed for the set. The positive emotions would be the fun colors such as lavender, pink, and yellow. The negative emotions would be represented by the boring, dark colors like brown and black. But you need all the colors to paint a masterpiece. If you don't use any dark colors, your painting wouldn't stand out. The fun colors would just blur together, and it would be void of accents. Similarly, a range of emotions is necessary to create a complete masterpiece of life.

Parenthood is always a roller coaster of emotions. Parents are filled with excitement and love from the moment of their child's birth, but other emotions creep in when the two-year-old child uses a permanent marker to draw on a freshly painted living room wall. Parents can experience the negative emotions of fear and worry when their teenager stays out past curfew, but the positive emotions are center stage when watching their adult daughter walk down the aisle.

Having a chronically ill child doesn't change the spectrum of parenthood emotions. We still experience a life full of fun and dark colored emotions. When we have more responsibilities, our perspective shifts, but we are still working with the same palette of available colors. We wouldn't want it to be different. I am grateful for it all. I wanted to cry when my daughter was upset because she just wanted to be a kid and not think about diabetes. I now know my broken heart in that moment was really my heart expanding to make room for the love it needed when she got accepted to medical school and became engaged. Feeling the negative emotions help us to fully feel and appreciate the positive emotions.

We need every emotion to be able to live a full, complete life. Labeling an emotion as positive or negative doesn't mean it shouldn't exist, but instead it tells us where it is on the spectrum of feelings. The secret to living a full life is learning to feel and process emotions. We absolutely have control over how we feel and that ultimately results in a masterpiece.

Acknowledgments

I am forever grateful to my patients who have allowed me to be a part of their lives and trust me with their care. The names of some patients were changed to respect their privacy.

I have chosen the Buddhist symbol called the unalome to represent my book. It is a symbol that represents the path to enlightenment, also represented by the gold color. The unalome embodies our experience as human beings on Earth and signifies a deeper awareness of how we move through life and learn from our actions. The twists and turns of life always create a straight path to our goals.

TO MY READERS:

Thank you for taking the time to read my book!
I really appreciate all of your feedback and
I love hearing what you have to say.

Please consider sharing it with friends and
family, but also take two minutes now to leave a
helpful review on Amazon letting me know what
you thought of the book:

maureenmichelemd.com/reclaiminglife

Thanks so much!

xo,

Maureen Michele, MD

www.ingramcontent.com/pod-product-compliance
Lightning Source LLC
Chambersburg PA
CBHW070706130626
46553CB00005B/1865